The Future of Water in African Cities

The Future of Water in African Cities

Why Waste Water?

Michael Jacobsen, Michael Webster,
and Kalanithy Vairavamoorthy
Editors

THE WORLD BANK
Washington, D.C.

WATER
PARTNERSHIP
PROGRAM

Contents

Boxes

Figures

Tables

Foreword

The management of water resources and supply is essential to the development and growth of cities. Sustainable resource use and the provision of quality services to a growing urban population underpins the success of future cities, enables them to act as poles of economic growth, and is at the core of social and economic development in an urbanizing world. The purpose of this book is to contribute to the broader green and inclusive growth ideas of the World Bank, by changing the way urban policy makers in Africa and project managers from the World Bank and other international organizations think about urban water management, planning, and project design.

The city of the future in Africa needs to be designed to accommodate twice as many people, and we need to plan it now. Traditional approaches are unlikely to be able to close the gap between supply and demand for water. Helping practitioners and decision makers in African cities consider a wider range of solutions to secure urban resilience in an uncertain future will require a concerted effort across sectors and institutions. Implementing efficient and flexible urban water systems and adopting a holistic view of all components of the urban water cycle will be essential if we want to provide environmentally sustainable growth and access to better services for current and future African communities.

Thanks to its flexibility and adaptability to a range of current and future conditions, Integrated Urban Water Management (IUWM) can be a powerful tool to provide clean safe water to African urban communities. It reflects the need to do things differently with the resources and expertise already at hand. IUWM is by no means a silver bullet that will solve all of Africa's urban water problems: the reforms it entails will be challenging, and its ideas and approaches will require testing on the ground. But as this book demonstrates, because it proposes to build systems incrementally and with broad consultation from stakeholders, the IUWM approach is, by nature, pragmatic and adaptive, and can help build green and inclusive growth in Africa.

Rachel Kyte
Vice President
Sustainable Development Network
World Bank

Makthar Diop
Vice President
Africa Region
World Bank

Acknowledgments

This report was edited by Michael Jacobsen (Senior Water Resources Specialist, World Bank), Michael Webster (Senior Water and Sanitation Specialist, World Bank), and Kalanithy Vairavamoorthy (Director, Patel School of Global Sustainability, University of South Florida or USF), with support from Daniel Shemie (Junior Professional Associate, World Bank), Alvar Closas (Consultant, World Bank), and Meleesa Naughton (Junior Professional Associate, World Bank). Each of the chapters was prepared by a group of authors, who in turn have drawn on key source documents that were commissioned from consultants and World Bank staff specifically for this work.

Chapter 1—Author: Michael Webster (Senior Water and Sanitation Specialist, World Bank)

Background material contributed by: Carolina Dominguez Torres (Consultant, World Bank), Gabrielle Puz (Consultant, World Bank), Nagaraja Rao Harshadeep (Senior Environmental Specialist, World Bank), and Asmita Tiwari (Consultant, World Bank)

Chapter 2—Authors: Kalanithy Vairavamoorthy (Director, Patel School of Global Sustainability, USF), Kebreab Ghebremichael (Senior Research Fellow, USF), Michael Jacobsen (Senior Water Resources Specialist,

World Bank), Jochen Eckart (Research Fellow, USF), Seneshaw Tsegaye (Research Fellow, USF), and Krishna Khatri (Research Fellow, USF)

Background material contributed by: Robin Bloch (Principal Consultant, GHK)

Chapter 3—*Authors*: Michael Jacobsen (Senior Water Resources Specialist, World Bank), and Alvar Closas (Consultant, World Bank)

Background material contributed by: Alvar Closas (Consultant, World Bank), Daniel Shemie (Junior Professional Associate, World Bank), Meleesa Naughton (Junior Professional Associate, World Bank), James Duncan (Consultant, World Bank), Brian Blankespoor (Environmental Specialist, World Bank), Ryan Engstrom (Assistant Professor, George Washington University), and Alyssa McCluskey (Senior Research Associate, University of Colorado)

Chapter 4—*Authors*: Michael Jacobsen (Senior Water Resources Specialist, World Bank), Gabrielle Puz (Consultant), and Daniel Shemie (Junior Professional Associate)

Background material contributed by: Kalanithy Vairavamoorthy (Director, Patel School of Global Sustainability, USF), Kebreab Ghebremichael (Senior Research Fellow, USF), Jochen Eckart (Research Fellow, USF), Seneshaw Tsegaye (Research Fellow, USF), Krishna Khatri (Research Fellow, USF), Barbara Anton (Project Coordinator, ICLEI—Local Governments for Sustainability), Ralph Philip (Project Officer, ICLEI), Murray Biedler (Consultant, ICLEI), João Rabaca (Consultant, ICLEI), Harrison Mutikanga (Manager, National Water and Sewerage Corporation or NWSC, Uganda), Joshua Oyieko (Consultant, ICLEI), Rose Kaggwa (Manager, NWSC), and Frank Kizito (Decision-Support Systems Manager, NWSC)

Chapter 5—*Authors*: Michael Jacobsen (Senior Water Resources Specialist, World Bank) and Michael Webster (Senior Water and Sanitation Specialist, World Bank)

Appendixes—*Authors:* Appendix 1: Alvar Closas (Consultant, World Bank), Dan Schemie (Junior Professional Associate, World Bank), Michael Jacobsen (Senior Water Resources Specialist, World Bank). Appendix 2: Alvar Closas (Consultant, World Bank), Michael Jacobsen (Senior Water Resources Specialist, World Bank), Meleesa Naughton (Junior Professional Associate, World Bank). Appendix 3: Alvar Closas (Consultant, World Bank), Michael Jacobsen (Senior Water Resources Specialist, World Bank), Meleesa Naughton (Junior Professional Associate, World Bank).

Appendix 4: James Duncan (Consultant, World Bank), Brian Blankespoor (Environmental Specialist, World Bank), Ryan Engstrom (Assistant Professor, George Washington University), and Christopher Marques (Consultant, World Bank)

This work was made possible by the financial contribution of the Water Partnership Program (WPP) (http://water.worldbank.org/water/wpp). The author team was inspired and supported throughout by Jamal Saghir (Director, Africa Sustainable Development Department, World Bank), Marianne Fay (Chief Economist, Sustainable Development Network, World Bank), José Luis Irigoyen (Director, Transport, Water, Information and Communication Technology Department, World Bank), Julia Bucknall (Manager, Water Anchor, World Bank), Ashok Subramanian (who initially proposed this Economic and Sector Work as former manager, Africa Water Resources, World Bank), Jonathan Kamkwalala (Manager, Africa Water Resources, World Bank), Junaid Kamal Ahmad (former Manager, Africa Region Urban and Water Unit, or AFTUW, World Bank), Alex Bakalian (Acting Sector Manager, AFTUW, World Bank), Idah Pswarayi-Riddihough (Sector Manager, Environment and Natural Resources Management, Africa Region, World Bank), and Jaehyang So (Manager, Water and Sanitation Program, World Bank).

Invaluable support for maps and databases was provided by Brian Blankespoor (Environmental Specialist, World Bank) and Jim Duncan (Consultant, World Bank), who were in turn supported by Ryan Engstrom (Assistant Professor, George Washington University) and Christopher Marques (Consultant, World Bank). The comprehensive and rigorous editorial support of Hilary Gopnik was very much appreciated. Meghana Kandekhar provided design support for graphics and Kristine Kelly for copyediting. Chonlada Sae-Hau and Immaculate Bampadde provided administrative assistance.

The authors would like to acknowledge the importance of the contributions of peer reviewers. External peer reviewers include Muchadeyi Masunda (His Worship the Mayor of Harare, Zimbabwe), Jean Pierre Mbassi (Secretary General, United Cities and Local Governments of Africa, or UCLGA), Sylvain Usher (Secretary General, African Water Association), Jay Bhagwan (Director, Water Use and Waste Management, Water Research Commission, South Africa), and Mark Pascoe (CEO, International Water Center, Australia). Internal peer reviewers include Daniel A. Hoornweg (Lead Urban Specialist, World Bank), Dominick Revell de Waal (Senior Economist, World Bank), David Michaud (Senior

Water and Sanitation Specialist, World Bank), Marcus J. Wishart (Senior Water Resources Specialist, World Bank), and Sudipto Sarkar (Sector Leader, World Bank).

A large number of colleagues and other professionals have contributed their advice and suggestions to the report. For the Nairobi case studies we thank Wambui Gichuri (Principal Regional Team Leader, Water and Sanitation Program, World Bank), Rafik Hirjii (Senior Water Resources Specialist, World Bank), Patrick Mwangi (Senior Water and Sanitation Specialist, World Bank), Pascaline Ndungu (Consultant, World Bank), Christian Peter (Senior Natural Resources Management Specialist, World Bank), Andreas Rohde (Senior Sanitary Engineer, World Bank), Rosemary Rop (Water and Sanitation Specialist, World Bank), and Johannes Zutt (Country Director, World Bank). For the Arua and Mbale case studies we thank Mukami Kariuki (Sector Leader, World Bank), Samuel Mutono (Senior Water and Sanitation Specialist, World Bank), Ahmadou Moustapha Ndiaye (Country Manager, World Bank), Halla Qaddumi (Consultant, World Bank), Adolf Spitzer (Senior Infrastructure Planner, NWSC), and Berina Uwimbabazi (Water Resources Management Specialist, World Bank).

This study would not have been possible without access to and interpretation of data provided by Alexander Danilenko (International Benchmarking Network for Water and Sanitation Utilities) and Rosemary Rop (Water Operators' Partnership—Africa, Water and Sanitation Program). In addition to the background material mentioned for each chapter, contributions to unpublished background papers and suggestions and comments on early drafts and ideas were provided by a large number of colleagues and professionals, including Ger Bergkamp (Director, International Water Association, or IWA), Greg Browder (Lead Water and Sanitation Specialist, World Bank), Uwe Deichman (Senior Environmental Specialist, World Bank), Martin Gambrill (Senior Water Engineer, World Bank), Abhas Jha (Lead Urban Specialist, World Bank), Felix Masangai (Head of Program, Ministry of Finance, Mozambique), Abel Mejia (Consultant, World Bank), David Michaud (Senior Water and Sanitation Specialist, World Bank), Soma Ghosh Moulik (Senior Water and Sanitation Specialist, World Bank), Ngoni Mudege (Consultant, Water and Sanitation Program), Paul Reiter (Executive Director, IWA), Matthijs Schuring (Operations Analyst, World Bank), Somnath Sen (Consultant, World Bank), Sarah Tibatemwa (Director, IWA Africa), Hyoung Wang (Economist, World Bank), and Tony Wong (Centre for Water Sensitive Cities, Monash University, Melbourne, Victoria, Australia).

About the Editors

Michael Jacobsen is currently a Senior Water Resources Specialist with the Water Anchor of the World Bank. He has published on water and climate change and is working with the interface between water resources, water services, economic growth, and urban planning. Prior to joining the World Bank in 2009, he was Chief Economist at a major engineering consultancy firm responsible for a number of environmental infrastructure projects and publishing on water tariffs (for the European Bank for Reconstruction and Development) and economic analysis of water projects (for the International Water Association). Mr. Jacobsen holds an MA in Economics from the University of Copenhagen.

Michael Webster is a Senior Water and Sanitation Specialist in the Africa Region of the World Bank. He is located in Zimbabwe and leads operations in Malawi, Zambia, and Zimbabwe in the water and urban sectors. During his 12 years at the Bank, he has worked on more than 40 operations in Africa, Asia, and Europe, and has lead analytical work on public finance and water. Prior to joining the Bank, he worked as an engineer and project manager in South Africa and the United Kingdom. Mr. Webster holds a BSc in Civil Engineering from the University of Cape Town, an MSc in Engineering from Loughborough University, and an MPP from Princeton.

Kalanithy Vairavamoorthy is an expert on urban water issues who has worked to create clean and sustainable water and sanitation systems through programs for the United Nations Educational, Scientific and Cultural Organization and the European Union. He currently directs the Patel School of Global Sustainability at the University of South Florida. In his career, Mr. Vairavamoorthy has led groups of researchers studying the future of sustainable water systems for cities and how urban areas might respond to water issues in the face of climate change and population growth. His current research includes development of new techniques for the flexible design of urban water supply systems operating under uncertainties associated with global change; application of optimization techniques for the operation and maintenance and life-cycle management of urban water systems; and development of risk assessment approaches for the design of sustainable urban water systems operating in the "city of the future."

Abbreviations

AfDB	African Development Bank
AfWA	African Water Association
AICD	Africa Infrastructure Country Diagnostic
AMCOW	African Ministers' Council on Water
BSWC	Borno State Water Corporation, Nigeria
BWB	Blantyre Water Board, Malawi
CSO	Country status overview
CWSC	Chipata Water and Sewerage Company, Zambia
DEWATS	Decentralized wastewater treatment systems
DWAF	Department of Water Affairs, South Africa
EU	European Union
GDP	Gross domestic product
GHK	GHK Consulting Limited
IBNET	International Benchmarking Network for Water and Sanitation Utilities
ICLEI	International Council for Local Environmental Initiatives
IDP	Integrated Development Plan, South Africa
ISO	International Organization for Standardization
IUWM	Integrated urban water management
IWA	International Water Association
IWRM	Integrated water resources management

KAP	Knowledge, attitudes, and practices
KIWASCO	Kisumu Water and Sewerage Company, Kenya
LAC	Latin America and Caribbean
LWSC	Lusaka Water and Sewerage Company, Zambia
Ml	Megaliter (one million liters)
MWSC	Mombasa Water and Sewerage Company, Kenya
NGWRP	New Goreangab Water Reclamation Plant, Namibia
NWASCO	Nairobi City Water and Sewerage Company, Kenya
NWSC	National Water and Sewerage Corporation, Uganda
OECD	Organisation for Economic Co-operation and Development
OGWRP	Old Goreangab Water Reclamation Plant, Namibia
ONEA	*Office Nationale des Eaux et Assainissement*, Burkina Faso
PAD	Project appraisal document
SAT	Soil aquifer treatment
SDE	*Sénégalaise des Eaux*, Senegal
SONEB	*Société Nationale des Eaux du Benin*, Benin
SNP	Slum Network Project, India
SWITCH	Sustainable Water Management Improves Tomorrow's Cities Health
TdE	*Togolaise des Eaux*, Togo
UCLGA	United Cities and Local Governments of Africa
UNDESA	United Nations Department of Economic and Social Affairs
UNDP	United Nations Development Programme
UNEP	United Nations Environment Programme
UNESCO	United Nations Educational, Scientific and Cultural Organization
UNESCO-IHE	United Nations Educational, Scientific and Cultural Organization, Institute for Water Education
UNESCO-IHP	United Nations Educational, Scientific and Cultural Organization, International Hydrological Programme
UN-HABITAT	United Nations Human Settlements Programme
UNICEF	United Nations Children's Fund
USF	University of South Florida
WBI	World Bank Institute
WHO	World Health Organization
WSP	Wastewater stabilization pond
WSS	Water supply and sanitation

Overview

The overall goal of this book is to change the way urban policy makers think about urban water management, planning, and project design in Africa. African cities are growing quickly, and their current water management systems cannot keep up with growing demand. It will take a concerted effort on the part of decision makers across sectors and institutions to find a way to provide sustainable water services to African city dwellers. This book argues that these complex challenges require innovative solutions and a management system that can work across institutional, sectoral, and geographic boundaries. A survey conducted for this analysis shows that African city leaders and utility operators are looking for ways to include a broader range of issues—such as water resources management, flood and drought preparation, rainwater harvesting, and solid waste management—than previously addressed in their water management plans. This book argues that integrated urban water management (IUWM) will help policy makers in African cities consider a wider range of solutions, understand water's interaction with other sectors, and secure resilience under a range of future conditions.

IUWM seeks to develop efficient, flexible, urban water systems by adopting a holistic view of all components of the urban water cycle (water supply, sanitation, stormwater management) in the context of the wider watershed. IUWM is formulated in response to the complexity of urban water management challenges worldwide. It addresses the key technical and institutional aspects of planning and design. The key to IUWM is integration at each stage of the planning process. Thus planners should consider the full range of challenges related to water management and their interactions within cities and the wider watershed, addressing issues such as:

- How is upstream land use and irrigation impacting water availability and quality downstream?
- How will future urban development impact water management challenges?
- Are pit latrines and poor sanitation conditions contaminating groundwater?
- Is solid waste clogging drains and thus causing flooding?

Decision makers must also consider a broad range of solutions to these problems, including the following:

- Do institutions adequately consider urban needs and impacts in terms of the broader watershed?
- Can alternative water sources such as rainwater harvesting, greywater recycling, and groundwater be harnessed in addition to traditional surface-water sources?
- Is water quality optimized for its intended use (such as drinking, irrigation, and manufacturing)?
- Can wastewater be exploited to produce cost-efficient energy?

Because both the challenges and solutions cross geographic and institutional boundaries, IUWM can only be implemented if institutions agree to work together. Examples of concerns that span such boundaries include making sure building codes do not impede rainwater harvesting, addressing health regulations that prevent greywater reuse, and ensuring that urban planners consider water management issues. IUWM understands that both the devil and the angel are in the details: each plan is formulated in consultation with local stakeholders—including the end users—to ensure that solutions are adapted to local conditions. Solutions are designed to be flexible—to handle the diversity of current conditions—and adaptive—to respond to the uncertain conditions of the future. In other words, IUWM is about doing things differently, rather than about doing different things.

The Challenge

Africa is urbanizing fast. Over the next 20 years, Africa's urban population will double. At 3.9 percent per year, urban population growth rates in Africa have been and will continue to be the highest in the world. Currently about 320 million Africans live in urban areas (37 percent of the African population), more than twice as many as in 1990. By 2030, Africa's urban population is forecast to rise to almost 50 percent of the population, or some 654 million people.

Demand for water is growing. Population growth in cities is driving this demand, but economic growth will add to it. More industry requires more water, and prosperity raises expectations for the quality of water services. A projected increase in the size of the middle class might lead to a demand for better governance and better services including more water services (World Bank, 2012). And water use outside cities, for agriculture and power, will grow even faster, putting more pressure on dwindling water resources. When these pressures are combined, it is projected that over the next 25 years the demand for water in Africa will almost quadruple—a much faster rate than any other region in the world (2030 Water Resources Group, 2009).

Water supply is shrinking, and water quality is deteriorating. As water demand grows, cities are forced to rely on water sources that are further from the city—and more expensive to tap. Land use changes upstream, including increasing informal irrigation and industry, have altered the seasonal pattern of runoff: there is more flooding in the wet season and less, but more turbid, water in the dry season. Groundwater might provide an alternate source of water, but poor sanitation threatens groundwater sources. Climate change will add uncertainty to this already precarious future for African water resources. Source protection, addressing water allocation issues, and improved wastewater management need to be part of any solution.

Water catchment issues are being felt in cities that did not expect it. Mbale, Uganda, one of the case studies in this book, is located in a high precipitation area at the foot of Mount Elgon, where surface water availability has traditionally been plentiful. Yet the city had to ration water in February 2012 for the first time, as one of its river sources dried up, and turbidity increased in the other. People—moving up the mountain in response to population pressure—were watering their gardens from mountain streams, leaving less water for the city downstream. This kind of increased competition for water in a catchment is happening throughout Africa, and the consequences are now felt in cities that did not imagine they would face shortages.

Despite successes, African cities have difficulty meeting the water challenge today. Between 2000 and 2010, 83 million urban Africans gained access to improved water and 42 million gained access to improved sanitation. But urban population increases moderated these successes, leaving the share of the population with access to improved water and sanitation unchanged at 83 percent and 43 percent respectively. Given the compound challenge of increases in demand for water and decreases in traditional supply sources, it is unlikely that the traditional approach of one source, one system, and one discharge can close the water gap.

Opportunities for Change

Challenges provide opportunities. Africa's rapid growth means that half of the city of 2035 has not yet been built. New water management systems may not be burdened with old infrastructure or approaches. Now is the time to plan for the future using state-of-the-art technologies and innovative management systems. The diverse, integrated approaches proposed in this book could lead to a major change in just 20 years. More importantly, these approaches are by nature flexible and adaptive. Because they tend to work on a smaller scale and account for the links between sectors, these methods can accommodate a broader range of future conditions than a traditional, centralized system. Given the uncertainties about the future growth patterns and climate conditions of African cities, this flexibility is a critical asset of an integrated approach to water management.

This book argues that a more integrated, sustainable, and flexible approach is needed in Africa, wanted by African city leaders, and is implementable. The first steps to implementation include demonstration projects, transfer of knowledge from other regions, and modification of the way urban water projects are planned, designed, and realized. This study conducted a review of the challenges and capacity of 31 cities in Africa. Water-related capacities and challenges were assessed relative to other African cities. Most of the cities with relatively large challenges also have relatively high capacity (see Figure 1), although this capacity might still be low compared to the daunting nature of the challenges. These cities might be ready to begin a dialogue about the applicability of IUWM for their water needs. Other cities clearly need to build capacity as a first step toward managing their water in a more integrated way.

Figure 1   Urban Water Management Challenges versus Institutional and Economic Capacities

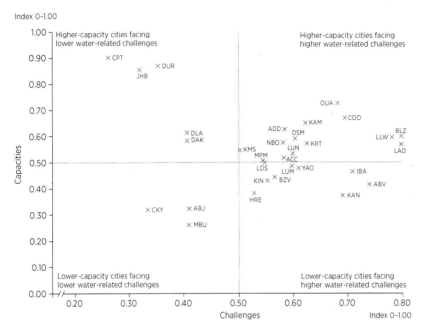

Index 0–1.00

Source: World Bank.
Note: City abbreviations: ABJ, Abidjan, Côte d'Ivoire; ABV, Abuja, Nigeria; ACC, Accra, Ghana; ADD, Addis Ababa, Ethiopia; BLZ, Blantyre, Malawi; BZV, Brazzaville, Republic of Congo; CKY, Conakry, Guinea; COO, Cotonou, Benin; CPT, Cape Town, South Africa; DAK, Dakar, Senegal; DLA, Douala, Cameroon; DSM, Dar es Salaam, Tanzania; DUR, Durban, South Africa; HRE, Harare, Zimbabwe; IBA, Ibadan, Nigeria; JHB, Johannesburg, South Africa; KAM, Kampala, Uganda; KAN, Kano, Nigeria; KIN, Kinshasa, Democratic Republic of Congo; KMS, Kumasi, Ghana; KRT, Khartoum, Sudan; LAD, Luanda, Angola; LLW, Lilongwe, Malawi; LOS, Lagos, Nigeria; LUM, Lubumbashi, Democratic Republic of Congo; LUN, Lusaka, Zambia; MBU, Mbuji-Mayi, Democratic Republic of Congo; MPM, Maputo, Mozambique; NBO, Nairobi, Kenya; OUA, Ouagadougou, Burkina Faso; YAO, Yaoundé, Cameroon.

Note on methodology: The figure presents an index that categorizes cities in two dimensions: water-related challenges and institutional and economic capacities. For each dimension, a number of variables were identified, for which indicators were then selected. For the water-related challenges dimension, indicators were selected for the following variables: urbanization challenges, solid waste management, water supply services, sanitation services, flood hazards, and water resources availability. For the institutional and economic capacities dimension, indicators were selected for the following variables: country policies and institutions, economic strength, water-related institutions, and water utility governance. Indicators were normalized, thus unit values vary from 0 to 1. Indicators were assigned equal weights and aggregated for each dimension. For further details, see Appendixes 2 and 3.

The book provides examples of cities in Africa and beyond that have already implemented IUWM approaches both in terms of technical and institutional solutions. A number of cities in Latin America have successfully developed innovative solutions that could be inspirational for African cities. Inspired by earlier work by the World Bank in Latin America, this book chose three cities, Nairobi (Kenya), and Mbale and

Arua (Uganda), as case studies for a more in-depth analysis of the applicability of IUWM to their water needs. Upon completion of this study, officials from all three cities expressed interest in implementing practical demonstration projects that would make use of some of the IUWM options presented in the book.

Water systems are complex; managers need to account for the interactions between urban water systems and the catchment from which they draw. The various components of the urban water system (water supply, wastewater, and stormwater) have a number of positive and negative interactions that reach beyond the water services sector. Horizontal integration of planning and integration across spatial boundaries is needed to improve services in a sustainable manner and to reduce vulnerabilities. Urban water systems depend increasingly on their water catchment for both quality and quantity of supply. And a city's water withdrawals and wastewater outputs, in turn, have a huge effect on the catchment from which they draw. Heredia in Costa Rica (66,000 water customers), like Mbale, is located at the foot of a mountain. It is able to supply its citizens with water with no other treatment than chlorination due to a payment for an environmental services agreement with landowners upstream. While these payments might require specific conditions to be effective, source protection and watershed management are becoming urban water issues throughout Africa.

Negative system interactions can be addressed with an integrated approach. The impact of poor sanitation on the water quality of potential water sources is an ongoing problem in many African cities. Other cities have successfully addressed this problem. In Indore, India, which has a population of 2 million, the Slum Network Project substantially upgraded the quality of life in slums through the creation of wastewater infrastructure that significantly improved the overall slum environment. But it did more. By looking at the larger picture, these improvements to the slum areas were also able to improve the water quality in the rest of the city, due to sewage no longer being dumped into rivers and streams. The costs of the system were the same as constructing pit latrines, but the overall results were better for people who lived in the slums, and better for the city as a whole (Diacon, 1997). In Latin America, the use of IUWM approaches made it apparent that reducing the blockage of drains from poor waste collection had a bigger impact on flooding than constructing new stormwater drains.

Positive system interactions can be exploited. There are opportunities for considering a portfolio of water sources, reuse, recycling, and cascading use in African cities. In Accra, Ghana, irrigated urban vegetable production provides up to 90 percent of the vegetable needs of the city (Tettey-Lowor, 2009). Most of the agricultural sites are located on valley bottoms along streams and drainage systems and use raw wastewater as the main source for irrigation. The research project called Sustainable Water Management Improves Tomorrow's Cities Health (SWITCH) developed institutional guidelines and piloted a low-cost treatment system to facilitate the safe reuse of wastewater for urban irrigation, while minimizing health risks.

Matching water quality to its intended function is the future in many cities, and the present in some. The one source, one system, and one discharge approach assumes that all water should be treated to the drinking water standard regardless of the purpose for which it will be used (human consumption, industrial use, or garden and park watering). This is an inefficient use of money, energy, and water. The concept of water that is fit to a purpose has been implemented in the city of Durban, South Africa, to respond to a conflict between water demand for domestic use and economic development under conditions of water scarcity. The eThekwini Water Services developed a strategy to recycle wastewater as an additional water source for industrial use. At operational capacity, the reclamation plant meets 7 percent of Durban's water demand and reduces the wastewater discharge by 10 percent. As a co-benefit, industrial customers reduce their costs by purchasing reclaimed water rather than high-quality, potable water.

Wastewater reuse needs to be considered, in particular where water is scarce. If water is scarce, then stormwater, greywater, and even wastewater are potentially economically attractive sources. Windhoek, Namibia, has an annual rainfall of only 350 millimeters, is 750 kilometers from the nearest perennial river, and is a rapidly growing city. Driven by these pressures, 26 percent of Windhoek's water supply comes from wastewater reuse—a system that has stood the city in good stead for decades. In the Arua case study carried out for this book, analysts propose a low-tech system to treat wastewater in the expanding outskirts of the city. The system would combine decentralized wastewater treatment systems (DEWATS) with soil aquifer treatment (SAT) to treat wastewater that replenishes groundwater, which is then reused for the potable water supply (see Figure 2). One alternative that has been seriously discussed for Arua is to take water from the Nile River, which is 40 kilometers away, and lift it 700 meters to serve the city (Eckart et al., 2012b). An IUWM approach might enable postponing the Nile River plan until the distant future.

Figure 2   Schematic of a Possible Integrated Water Supply and Sanitation System for a Future Development Area in Arua, Uganda

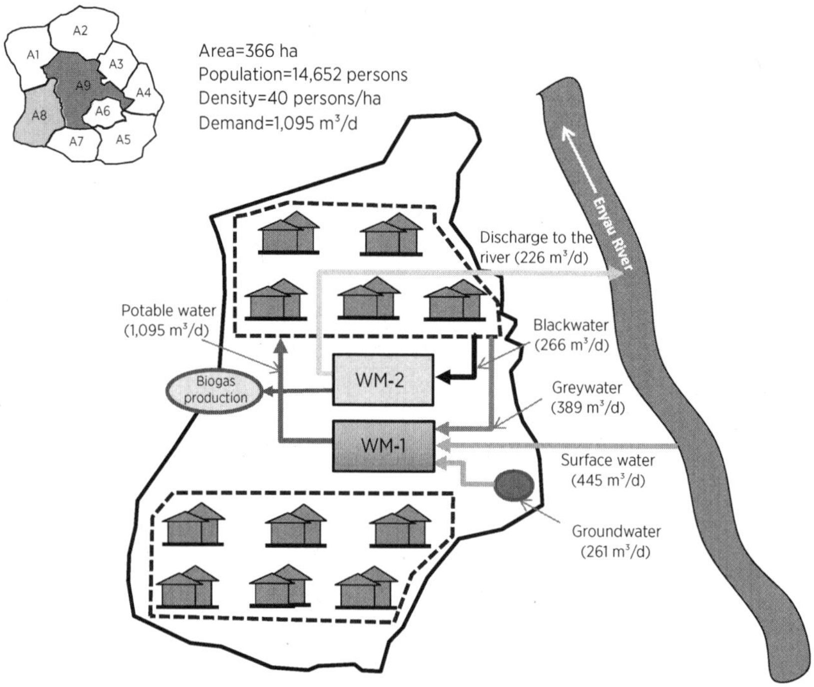

Area=366 ha
Population=14,652 persons
Density=40 persons/ha
Demand=1,095 m³/d

Discharge to the river (226 m³/d)

Potable water (1,095 m³/d)

Blackwater (266 m³/d)

Biogas production

WM-2

Greywater (389 m³/d)

WM-1

Surface water (445 m³/d)

Groundwater (261 m³/d)

Enyau River

Source: World Bank.
Note: The figure presents the different technologies used as part of the proposed water supply and sanitation system for a new planned development cluster in Arua (Uganda) as a typical example of an urban cluster with access to surface water for dilution. The top left hand corner figure shows the existing built-up area A9 in dark gray and the proposed development cluster A8 in light gray. Technologies used in water management (WM): WM-1: DEWATS with SAT and a conventional treatment unit (or with advanced treatment); WM-2: DEWATS. ha = hectares; m³/d = cubic meters per day.

A diversity of solutions provides flexibility. Big cities will continue to need big infrastructure. But an exclusive reliance on major infrastructure makes cities vulnerable. By relying on a limited number of surface-water sources to supply centralized systems, cities put themselves at risk of increased competition for water, climate variability, and political wrangling. Nairobi imports more than 80 percent of its water from other counties. With ongoing decentralization of political power in Kenya, it may become politically difficult and costly for Nairobi to continue to divert water from counties that themselves find it difficult to serve their populations. The Nairobi case study commissioned for this book illustrates that

Figure 3   Proposed Staged Development of Alternative Water Sources in Nairobi, Kenya, 2010 to 2035

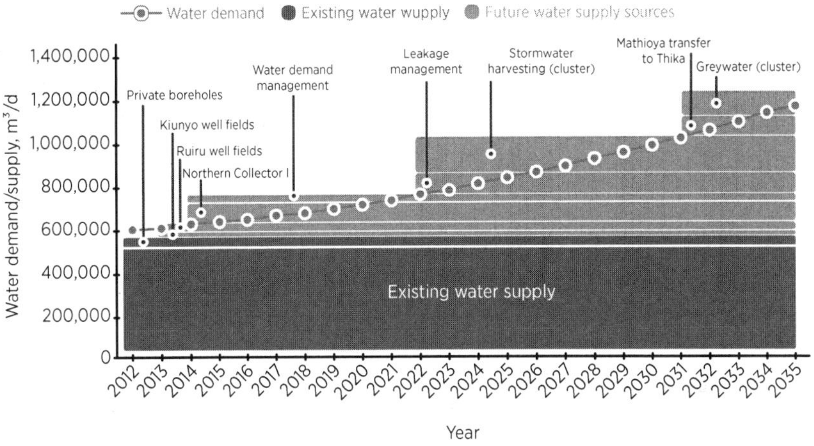

Source: World Bank.
Note: The figure shows the years at which the different water sources need to be developed to meet the growing water demand for Nairobi. The volume of water supplies from each source has been determined based on meeting medium-term water demand projections. Some of the sources might need to be developed at the same time (for example, Northern Collector 1 and water demand management; leakage management and stormwater harvesting). m³/d = cubic meters per day.

leakage reduction, water demand management, stormwater and rainwater harvesting, and greywater recycling may provide added flexibility and resilience (see Figure 3). Some of these sources are seasonal in nature, but with carefully designed storage facilities, such a solution may also provide additional resilience to prolonged droughts and climate change.

Horizontal integration of planning and integration across spatial boundaries is possible with a concerted effort and national support. Polokwane, the capital of Limpopo province in South Africa, has put in place a water strategy that emphasizes building capacity to strengthen the coordination of water use and supply, water safety plans for catchment areas, a drought management plan including increased use of recycled wastewater, demand management, as well as a pressure reduction system to reduce water leakage, and a price structure to encourage water savings.

Critical to the success of IUWM is the early and continuous involvement of all stakeholders—including the public—in the planning, decision-making, and implementation process. Stakeholder and public participation can improve the scope of decision making and can help to create long-term and widely acceptable solutions. It is important to ensure that decisions are soundly based on shared knowledge, experience, and evidence; that decisions are influenced by the views and experience of those affected by them; that innovative and creative options are considered; and that new arrangements are workable and acceptable to the public (European Commission 2002). In African cities these arguments are even more important than in a European setting. In view of the weak capacity to enforce planning and regulation, African cities will have to rely on self-enforcement to a large degree, which will require continuous public involvement, acceptance, and approval.

Other regions—and farsighted Africans—have already taken onboard the integrated approach. Responding to client demand, the World Bank's Latin America and the Caribbean (LAC) Region has worked for several years on an operational framework for stronger World Bank engagement in IUWM in Latin America (World Bank, 2010). There is a growing chorus of water professionals (IWA, 2010), municipal leaders (ICLEI, 2012), and academics (for example, see UNESCO-IHP, 2009 and SWITCH, 2011), arguing that a new approach to urban water management is needed. In the words of an African academic, "meeting urban water needs in the twenty-first century will require a paradigm shift. Nineteenth century supply side solutions alone will not balance the ever-growing demand for water driven by rapid urbanization, shortage of surface and ground water due to climate change, and competition from agriculture" (Awiti, 2012).

African city leaders agree that plans should be integrated—but currently they are not. As part of this book a knowledge, attitudes, and practices (KAP) survey asked city leaders of African municipalities and utilities about the scope of their current water management plans and about their opinions of what should be included in a future plan. While the current plans typically do not include drought and flooding contingencies, rainwater harvesting, or drainage and solid waste management, city leaders overwhelmingly agree that such issues should be included in water management plans (see Figure 4).

The World Bank Response

Is the World Bank water practice ready to respond to the African urban water management challenge with new ideas? This book suggests four avenues for the Bank's response: Increase the use of an IUWM approach in World Bank project planning and design; promote pilot programs to demonstrate IUWM in practice in cities that have expressed interest;

Figure 4   Responses to KAP Survey from Water Operators and Municipalities in Africa

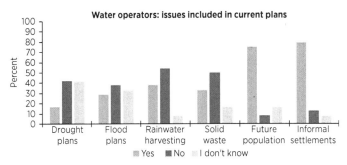

Water operators: issues included in current plans

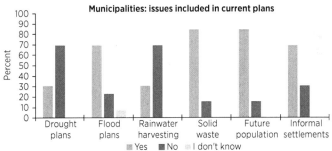

Municipalities: issues included in current plans

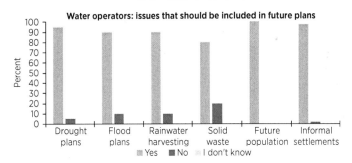

Water operators: issues that should be included in future plans

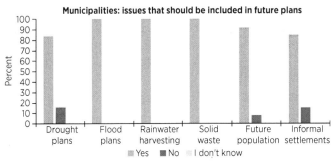

Municipalities: issues that should be included in future plans

Source: World Bank.
Note: See Appendix 1 for methodology.

undertake additional research on specific institutional and financial requirements and implications at the local level; and build a better understanding of what IUWM means in practice and at the local level through support of an IUWM learning alliance.

The World Bank should engage proactively with IUWM principles. Considering IUWM options should become a standard part of planning water projects, and they should be put into action where clients and staff agree on their utility. The Bank should provide technical assistance from its staff and consultants to IUWM projects, and can act as a facilitator to promote integrated water management in international forums.

Linking IUWM to investment projects is critical for success. Africa faces acute urban water management challenges. Unless IUWM is linked to investment projects, it is not likely to be perceived as relevant in Africa. It is time to move holistic thinking into the trenches of applied water management systems.

Demonstration projects are essential to raise awareness and better understanding of how IUWM could work in practice in Africa. In each of the three cities for which IUWM case studies were commissioned—Nairobi (Kenya), Mbale and Arua (Uganda)—authorities expressed a keen interest in implementing specific demonstration projects. In both countries World Bank urban and water projects are near implementation stage, and they could serve as a vehicle to move forward with demonstration projects.

This book argues that integration of decision making across sectors is critical for cities to cope with the challenges of rapid urban growth and a threatened water supply. Unfortunately, we don't know enough about the local-level institutional and financing implications of more integration. Additional research is required at the local and national levels to better understand how institutions can cope with the added responsibility of joint decision making. The World Bank can foster this research through interregional dialogue and support of knowledge building on the ground in Africa.

This book recommends collaboration with the International Water Association (IWA) and other networks in Africa to build an IUWM Network–Learning Alliance. Such a Network–Learning Alliance for Africa would support capacity development of personnel and institutions and would serve three main purposes: (1) the network would advocate the use of IUWM where appropriate; (2) it would serve as a liaison to share knowledge and technology; and (3) it would provide implementation support for providers of water management services. Basing a

Network–Learning Alliance in an existing organization (IWA) will make it more cost-efficient and sustainable.

Within the World Bank Group, the Water and Sanitation Program and the World Bank Institute would be important partners, but learning across Regions would also be essential. By its very nature an IUWM Network–Learning Alliance for Africa would be cross-sectoral. Within the World Bank it would, at a minimum, involve the Urban and Water networks in addition to the Africa Region. Close contacts with other parts of the Bank working on similar issues, such as the LAC Water Beam, would be crucial to maximize the ability of the Bank to draw globally on knowledge and centers of excellence.

IUWM is not a silver bullet that will solve all of Africa's urban water problems. Its ideas and approaches will require testing on the ground and in the sewers and pipes of African cities. Some will work well and some will be rejected. Some will be cost-efficient and some will be too expensive. But because it proposes to build systems incrementally and with broad consultation from stakeholders, the IUWM approach is by nature pragmatic. The flexibility of the options it proposes, and its adaptability to a range of current and future conditions, will be a powerful tool to provide clean, safe water to African communities.

CHAPTER 1

Africa's Emerging Urban Water Challenges

Africa's rapid urbanization will result in new water management challenges for cities. Over the next 20 years, the urban population of Sub-Saharan Africa (hereinafter "Africa") will double (UN-Habitat, 2011). This growth will bring opportunities to capitalize on the potential for economic expansion and challenges to avoid the many social problems, such as expanding slums, associated with unplanned urban growth. Effective water management will be critical in preparing cities to face this emerging challenge.

The gap between water demand and water supply is growing. Water demand is increasing at a higher rate than population growth—as income levels of urban dwellers rise and the demands for better services increase—whereas water availability is shrinking due to competing demands from agriculture, mining, and industry and from deteriorating water quality and climate change. Cities also face more flood hazards due to a complex web of land use, solid waste management, drainage, and wastewater management issues. The structure of urban growth in Africa and uncertainties of climate further add to the complexity of the challenges. African cities must sprint in order to stand still to meet the demands of rapid urban population growth.

Solving future urban water challenges is essential for growth and poverty reduction. Cities are the drivers of future economic growth through both the manufacturing and service sectors. The poor quality of infrastructure is a major constraint to doing business and to receiving foreign investment. Water scarcity harms production and hence income in cities, due to household and manufacturing coping strategies in the face of scarcity, extra abstraction costs, and lost production caused by intermittent energy supply due to hydropower disruptions. The urban poor are disproportionately affected by water rationing in a water crisis because they have no storage. Addressing Africa's urban water challenges will significantly improve the ability of cities (and countries) to maximize their economic growth and mitigate the rise of urban slums.

Africa's Rapid Urbanization Brings Opportunities and Threats

Africa is urbanizing quickly. Over the next 20 years, Africa's urban population will double. At 3.9 percent per year, urban population growth rates in Africa have been and will continue to be the highest in the world. Although Africa is currently the second least urbanized region (after South Asia), urbanization and urban growth are inversely correlated. Currently about 320 million Africans (37 percent of the population) live in urban areas, more than twice as many as in 1990. By 2030, Africa's urban population is forecast to rise to almost 50 percent of the population, or some 654 million people (see Figures 1.1 and 1.2). To put it another way, half the people who will be living in African cities 20 years from now have yet to arrive: now is the time for city planners to prepare for their arrival.

Econometric studies have consistently shown a strong correlation between urbanization and gross domestic product (GDP), and between urban growth and economic growth. No country has achieved middle-income status without urbanizing (World Bank, 2009). In Africa, urban household income is twice as high as rural household income. The economic growth that occurred in Africa in the 1990s and 2000s derived primarily from the industrial and service sectors, which are mainly urban-based (Kessides, 2006). Informal activity—estimated to account for 93 percent of all new jobs created and 61 percent of urban employment—significantly adds to the relative share of growth from the urban sphere.

Urban growth is highly correlated to growth in slums. Africa is urbanizing more quickly and has faster growing slums than any other region. Africa has a relatively small share of the global slum population (20 percent in 2005), but this proportion has increased from 14 percent in 1990 and slum populations doubled during those 15 years. The proportion of Africa's urban population living in slums has stayed the same (72 percent)

Figure 1.1   Trend in Urbanization in Africa

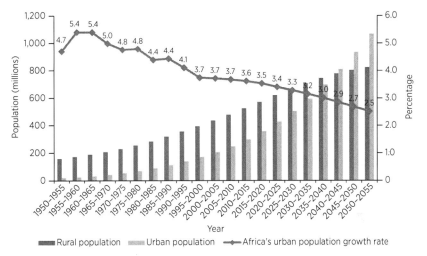

Source: UNDESA, 2012.

Figure 1.2   Level of Urbanization and Urban Population Growth Rates in Africa

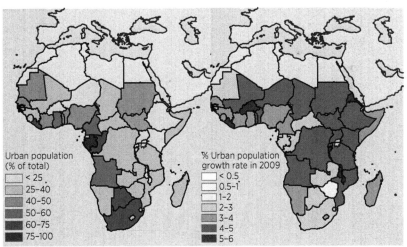

Sources: Maps produced by Africa Spatial Services Helpdesk based on World Bank, 2010a and 2011a.

whereas this proportion has dropped from 47 percent to 41 percent on average in other developing regions (see Figure 1.3 and Table 1.1).

Many large African cities are as dense as large Asian cities (see Figure 1.4). Density in the informally settled slum areas is particularly high. In

Figure 1.3   Population Living in Slums in Africa

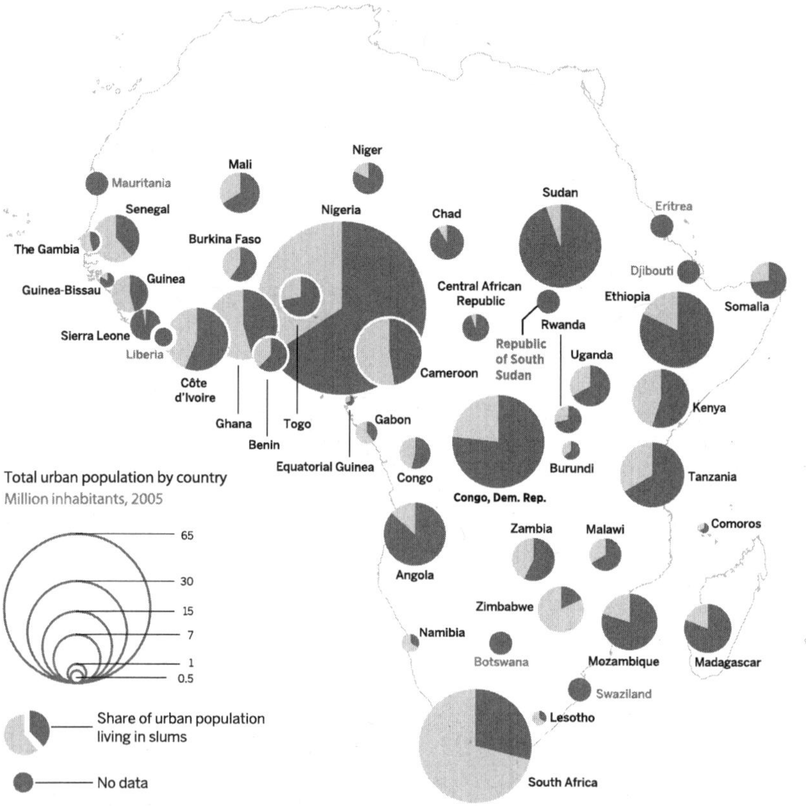

Source: World Bank, based on figure by Pravettoni and UNEP/GRID-Arendal, 2011 with data from UNDESA, 2010.

Table 1.1   Slum Population as a Share of Urban Population in Africa and the World

Location	Slum population, 1990 (millions)	Urban residents in slums, 1990 (%)	Slum population, 2005 (millions)	Urban residents in slums, 2005 (%)
World	715	31	998	31
Other developing countries	654	47	933	41
Sub-Saharan Africa	101	72	199	72

Source: UN-Habitat, 2006.

Figure 1.4   Density of 31 African Cities (Light) Compared to Reference Cities (Dark)

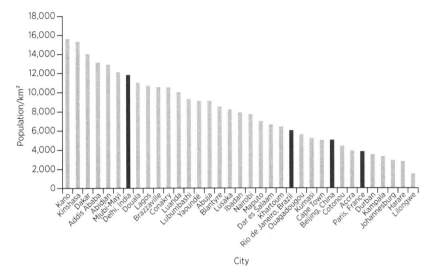

Source: Demographia, 2011. km^2= square kilometers.

addition to the institutional and financial challenges of working in informal settlements, crowding creates additional technical challenges: retrofitting infrastructure such as traditional sewer or water supply networks is difficult because there is not enough space to accommodate new equipment.

African Cities Struggle to Provide Access to Water and Sanitation to Their Current Population

In 2010, only 61 percent of Africans had access to clean water and 31 percent to adequate sanitation (WHO/UNICEF, 2012). In urban areas, the situation was slightly better with 83 percent access to water and 43 percent access to sanitation. Globally, the world will reach the Millennium Development Goals for water, but not for sanitation. However, in Africa, despite the significant number of people who have gained access to water since 1990, the Millennium Development Goals for water will not be reached.

Between 2000 and 2010, 84 million urban Africans gained access to improved water supply and 42 million to improved sanitation (see Table 1.2). This is an impressive 3.9 percent average increase in access over the decade. However, urban population also grew by an average of 3.9 per-

Table 1.2   Urban Population with Access to Water Supply and Sanitation 2000 and 2010 (in thousands)

	Population		Drinking water				Sanitation facilities			
	Urban	National	Urban improved		National improved		Urban improved		National improved	
Year	#	#	#	%	#	%	#	%	#	%
2000	217,803	668,379	179,482	82	367,661	55	92,917	43	185,808	28
2010	318,383	855,477	263,195	83	524,264	61	135,402	43	261,505	31

Source: WHO/UNICEF, 2012.

cent, so that the proportion of urban dwellers with access to water and sanitation services remained static.

Rapid urban growth is occurring throughout the continent, but access to water varies from country to country. In Uganda, the proportion of the urban population with access to improved water sources increased from 78 percent (1.5 million people) in 1990 to 91 percent (3.7 million) in 2008. During the same time period, in Nigeria access to water in urban areas fell from 79 percent (27 million) to 75 percent (55 million). Both countries managed to double the number of people with access to safe water, but in Nigeria the expansion could not keep up with population growth (WHO/UNICEF, 2012).

Utilities operate aging infrastructure aimed at supplying the city as it once was. About two-thirds of Africa's urban population is served by water utilities (AICD, 2011). Adequate funding is not available to utilities for expansion or renewal of aging infrastructure in African cities; compared to the rest of the world, the sector is underfunded (see Table 1.3).[1] Naturally, capital expenditures vary with incomes, but most of the utilities in our sample spend 10 times less on infrastructure renewal and expansion than the average for India.

Access and service quality vary between countries. In middle-income countries such as South Africa, utilities reach about 99 percent of the urban population, the vast majority through private piped water connections. In low-income countries, 49 percent of urban areas receive water from utilities and less than half of these are through piped connections. Informal sharing of connections between neighbors accounts for 15 percent and communal standpipes account for 19 percent of water distribution. In Maputo, Mozambique, one-third of unconnected households purchase water from their household neighbors, and in Maseru, Lesotho, household resellers provide water to 31 percent of the population, including almost half of the unconnected households (AICD, 2011).

Table 1.3   Annual Average Capital Expenditure for African Utilities

Utility	Average annual capital expenditure per person served (US$)	GDP per capita, 2006 (US$)	Operating ratio for latest available year (%)
KIWASCO (Kisumu, Kenya)	0.03	616	109
MWSC (Mombasa, Kenya)	0.13	616	107
CWSC (Chipata, Zambia)	0.19	911	—
BWB (Blantyre, Malawi)	0.20	236	106
NWASCO (Nairobi, Kenya)	0.23	616	100
SDE (Senegal)	0.24	839	240
SONEB (Benin)	0.66	602	196
LWSC (Lusaka, Zambia)	1.04	911	135
TdE (Togo)	1.14	398	45
NWSC (Uganda)	1.27	340	134
Average, India	3.06	822	n.a.
BSWC (Borno State, Nigeria)	3.49	1,015	—
Average, South-East Asia	7.02	—	n.a.
ONEA (Burkina Faso)	13.17	395	207
Average, Australia	165.80	36,226	n.a.

Sources: World Bank calculations based on AICD, latest available year; Asian Development Bank, 2007 and 2007a; IBNET, latest available year; Marsden and Pickering, 2006; Mugabi and Castro, 2009; and World Bank, 2006.
Note: Average annual capital expenditure is for 2001 to 2006 for African utilities, and 2000 to 2005 for Australian, Indian, and South-East Asian utilities. Values for Australian, Indian, and South-East Asian annual capital expenditures are averages for seven, twenty, and forty utilities, respectively. Conversion to U.S. dollars based on official exchange rate for the period average. Benchmark for operating ratio is 130 percent based on Banerjee and Morella, 2011. — = not available. n.a. = not applicable.

African water utilities often deliver poor continuity of water service and inadequate water quality (see Figure 1.5). Utilities report providing from 6 to 24 hours of service daily, and just over 80 percent of their samples pass chemical tests. The reliability of service varies greatly as does the water consumption per capita, from 240 liters per capita per day in Johannesburg to 7 liters per capita per day in the Central African Republic.

The numbers of households relying on boreholes and wells has increased by 22 million over the past decade, but infrastructure dilapidation and lack of well and borehole maintenance has rendered many of these sources unsuitable to secure safe drinking water. For instance, in the Central African Republic only 10 percent of the wells and boreholes provide safe water (Dominguez-Torres and Foster, 2011) despite these being the main source of water for urban dwellers.

Poor cost recovery and governance limits expansion of service coverage. It has been estimated that achievement of full cost recovery would

Figure 1.5   Water Consumption per Capita Supplied by Utility and Continuity of Piped Water Supply

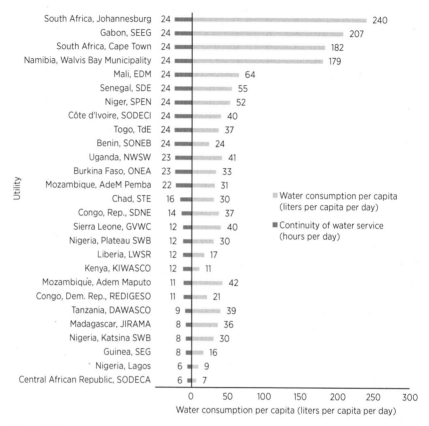

Source: AICD, 2011.
Note: Figure lists the country and name of the utility.

require stiff tariff increases for residential consumers. But in most African countries, only the rich are connected to the network, which might render this affordability argument politically convenient. Tariffs that fully recover capital costs would be affordable for only half of the population in Africa (Banerjee and Morella, 2011). Poor people currently pay many times the official water tariffs, as they buy their water from private providers. Recovering full costs from existing customers and using the resulting cash flow to increase access for the poor would substantially increase equity, although there are political issues that will be difficult to overcome (van Ginneken et al., 2012).

Access to water and sanitation services is unequal: piped water is available primarily to upper-income residents, while the poor rely on untreated wells and surface water (see Figure 1.6). Sanitation services are also dependent on income, with upper-income groups serviced with water-borne sewers, and the poor resorting to open defecation or traditional latrines.

Urban sanitation services serve fewer people than those served by piped water. A little more than half of the households with piped water also have flush toilets, which are often connected to septic tanks rather than to sewers. Namibia, Senegal, and South Africa report universal coverage by sewerage but in most other African countries, sewerage serves less than even 10 percent of urban areas (AICD, 2011). Improved latrines and septic tanks are used by the richest 20 to 40 percent of the population, but traditional pit latrines are the most common facility for most urban dwellers. While the share of urban population having to resort to open defecation is less than 10 percent (Dominguez-Torres, 2011), in peri-urban areas this figure is likely to be higher. Typically more than 40 percent of households share their toilets with others. This crowding causes maintenance problems and health issues (AICD, 2011).

Only a small proportion of wastewater is collected, and an even smaller fraction is treated. Outside South Africa, few cities have functioning wastewater treatment plants. Of the 11 cities that were assessed in the background paper on wastewater (World Bank, 2012c), only half had

Figure 1.6   Coverage of Water Services, by Budget Quintile

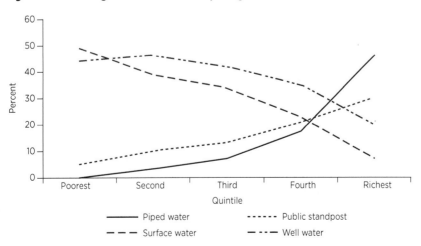

Source: AICD, 2011.

wastewater treatment plants (half of which were lagoon-based), and many of these were not functioning or functioning significantly below capacity. For example, in Luanda, a city of over 4 million, all the collected wastewater is discharged untreated into the sea outfall. Harare had a relatively high level of wastewater treatment 15 years ago, but now it is estimated that only 5 percent of the wastewater produced is treated in two large activated sludge plants and two waste stabilization ponds. Even in South Africa, which has an extensive network of wastewater treatment plants, of the 1,600 treatment plants operating, 60 percent do not meet discharge requirements (GWI, 2009).

Water Demand Increases Even Faster than Population Growth

The increase in water demand in Africa between 2005 and 2030 is projected to be 283 percent—three times higher than almost any other region (see Figure 1.7). A significant portion of this new demand (an estimated 92 billion cubic meters, or 20 percent) will come from the municipal and domestic sectors, and competition with other water-using sectors, most notably agriculture (which accounts for 72 percent of this increase), will increase dramatically.

Four factors account for increased urban water demand: growth in urban population; increase in industrial and commercial demand, linked

Figure 1.7   Increase in Annual Water Demand (2005 to 2030)

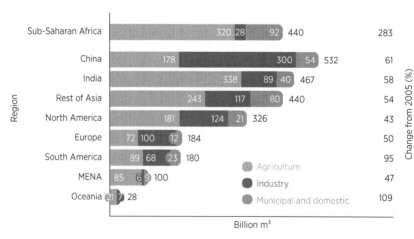

Source: World Bank, based on 2030 Water Resources Group, 2009.
Note: MENA: Middle East and North Africa. m³ = cubic meters.

to industrialization; rising incomes that increase expectations of water quantity and quality; and a growing middle class leading to improved governance and more market-oriented policies, which can result in demand for better services (World Bank, 2012). Increased pressures come with opportunities for improved water management policies and implementation.

Water Supply Depends on the Quantity and Quality of Water in the Catchment

While water demand grows, water resources are becoming scarcer (see Figure 1.8). More than 40 percent of Africans live in arid, semiarid, and dry subhumid areas. The amount of water available per person in Africa is far below the global average and is declining—with annual per capita availability of 4,000 cubic meters compared to a global average of 6,500 cubic meters (UNEP, 2010). Drought is endemic to many regions and repeated drought cycles kill thousands of people each year. In addition, the groundwater table is being lowered and rainfall is declining in many regions (UNEP, 2010). Africa has a large number of shared watersheds, which increases competition between states for limited resources. The increase in solid waste and wastewater generated by urban areas will place further pressure on water quality and on urban drainage, which will

Figure 1.8   Disappearing Lake Chad: A High-Profile Case of Diminishing Surface Water Sources, 1972 (Left) and 2007 (Right)

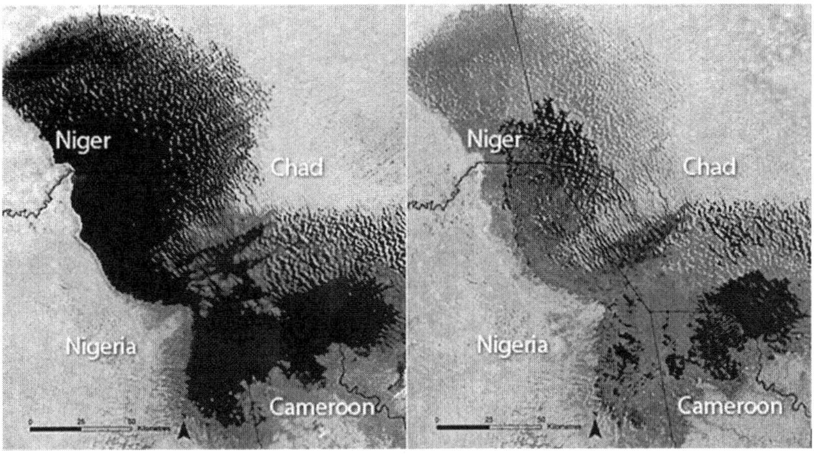

Source: UNEP, 2008.

further complicate efforts to secure an adequate supply of clean water to a thirsty population.

Africa has about 9 percent of the globe's fresh-water resources, but utilization is low in many basins. For example, less than 2 percent of the Congo River's tremendous water resources are used. Most water use in the continent is for agriculture, although domestic and industrial uses of water are growing near urban areas (UNEP, 2008).

Many countries in Africa have less fresh water per person than countries in the Middle East and Asia usually thought of as water scarce. A number of southern, eastern, and central African countries are water stressed or water scarce (see Figure 1.9).

Water extraction for irrigation and other uses in upstream catchments affects water flows downstream. Such changes in the hydrograph simultaneously increase the flood hazard in the rainy season and reduce the availability of perennial water supplies for cities in the dry season. The ability to deal effectively with the issue of watershed protection is often hampered by a multitude of institutions and the fact that the benefits and costs of watershed protection often accrue to different groups.

One possible solution to this problem is increased reliance on groundwater. Groundwater is a potential source of water for many water scarce areas where surface water is unavailable or too costly to tap. A recent report from the British Geological Society estimates that the groundwater available in aquifers in Africa is 100 times the amount found on the surface (MacDonald et al., 2011; McGrath, 2012).

Urban water source pollution is caused by inadequate sanitation, poor wastewater management, and seawater intrusion. In Dakar, Senegal, where about 80 percent of water comes from groundwater, contamination from nitrates and seawater intrusion is posing a serious threat to water quality (Bloch, 2012). Other African coastal capitals such as Abidjan, Dar es Salaam, Lagos, and Lomé suffer from similar groundwater contamination. The situation is equally acute in Harare, Zimbabwe, where the city's main water source, Lake Chivero, is being polluted by discharge of untreated wastewater and unregulated industrial pollution directly into the lake. The resultant pollutant load costs the city almost US$2 million per month in chemicals to treat the water, a prohibitive amount for a city that is struggling to provide basic services to its citizens.

Industrial pollution, particularly from mining, is an important but under-researched issue for many African cities. Mining-related pollution of ground and surface water can persist for many years—even after the activities have ceased—and should be considered in any watershed man-

Figure 1.9   Availability of Fresh Water per Person per Year by Country in 2007

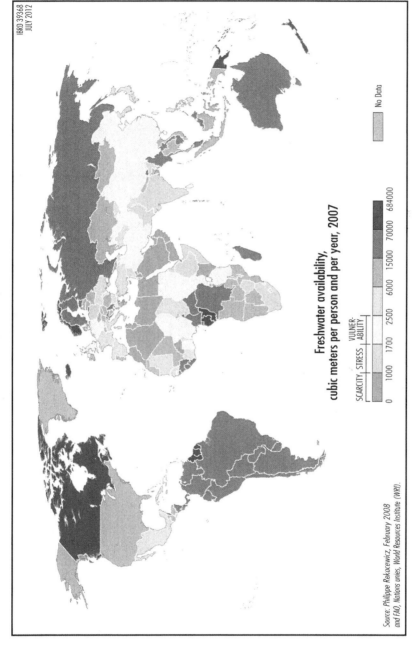

Freshwater availability,
cubic meters per person and per year, 2007

Source: Philippe Rekacewicz, February 2008 and FAO, Nations unies, World Resources Institute (WRI).

Source: Based on Rekacewicz, 2006.

27

agement plan. Cotonou in Benin, Accra in Ghana, and Lagos in Nigeria all suffer heavy pollution from industry (Bloch, 2012).

Poor Drainage and Flooding Are a Growing Problem

It has been shown in many cities around the world that poor solid waste management can impact urban drainage (UN-Habitat, 2010). A background paper completed for this study (Sen, 2012) found that while progress has been made in solid waste management in some African cities—including testing of different models of primary collection and disposal—little information is available on drainage. Serious episodes of flooding in African cities, however, show that drainage is conspicuous by its absence.

A lack of stormwater drainage infrastructure, blocked and poorly maintained stormwater drains, and settlements in previously unsettled low-lying areas have contributed to recurrent urban flooding in many African cities including Bangui, Central African Republic, and Dakar, Senegal. The large exposure to flood hazards and the vulnerability to floods is closely linked to inadequate planning of the urban space, poor access to more distant areas, and poor enforcement of existing regulations.

With additional development and possibly more severe storms due to climate change, cities could experience higher frequency, duration, and intensity of flooding events. Sea-level rise could increase the threat in coastal cities. More severe storms and increases in wastewater flows can exacerbate gully formation (as in southeastern Nigeria, see Figure 1.10). Gullies can undermine housing and infrastructure, threaten lives, and damage livelihoods.

Traditional solutions to drainage issues might not be sufficient. Solid waste management and drainage are typically a municipal responsibility and wastewater management a utility responsibility; institutional divisions make it difficult to implement plans that crosscut sectors, like those needed for urban drainage. Traditional drainage solutions (deep trenches) are also costly, energy intensive, and vulnerable to poor solid waste management solutions.

These Challenges Are Exacerbated by Climate Variability, Flooding, and Uncertainty about the Future

The new urban paradigm in Africa calls for an innovative urban planning and management approach that will allow cities to grow safely and ensure that residents suffer less damage from disasters. As the population

Figure 1.10   Buildings at Risk due to Gully Erosion, Omagba, Nigeria

Source: Nigeria Erosion and Watershed Management Project, World Bank (provided by Stephen Danyo).

swells in cities across Africa, now is the time to act to build resilient cities. Africa is exposed to multiple natural hazards, the intensity and impacts of which are likely to increase with climate change. Investing in disaster preparedness is critical for the lives and livelihoods of residents in times of crisis, as well as for ensuring a competitive city image necessary for attracting and sustaining economic activities.

Africa's climate is highly seasonal, and varies widely from year to year. The continent's climatic zones range from humid equatorial, to seasonally arid tropical, to subtropical Mediterranean climates. Each climatic zone exhibits different degrees of variability in rainfall and temperature. Hydrological variability and extremes are at the heart of the challenge of achieving basic water security in Africa. Year-to-year and decade-to-decade phenomena such as the El Niño Southern Oscillation also have a significant impact on African hydrology (Parry et al., 2007).

The high variability of precipitation and temperature across Africa translates into widely varying runoff, with basins such as the Congo displaying extremely high runoff and the arid and semiarid regions of Egypt, the Sahel, Sudan, and southern Africa displaying very low runoff. Much of Africa also exhibits significant changes in runoff and flows within and across years. Although annual variability in rainfall is high in most of

Africa, some regions, notably the Sahel, show substantial variability from decade to decade. By contrast, eastern and southeastern Africa show relatively stable patterns (Parry et al., 2007).

Africa's climatic and hydrologic variability is manifested as droughts and floods that destroy livelihoods and undermine economic progress (see Figure 1.11). Variability also discourages investment and encourages other risk-averse behavior that aggravates the poverty trap. It is no coincidence that in many of the world's poorest countries, climate variability is high, water-related investments are relatively limited, and there is often a strong correlation between rainfall variability and GDP, with GDP dropping 10 percent or more at times due to increasing rainfall variability. Most natural disasters in Africa are climate-related, and large areas

Figure 1.11   Current and Future Population in African Cities Exposed to Drought

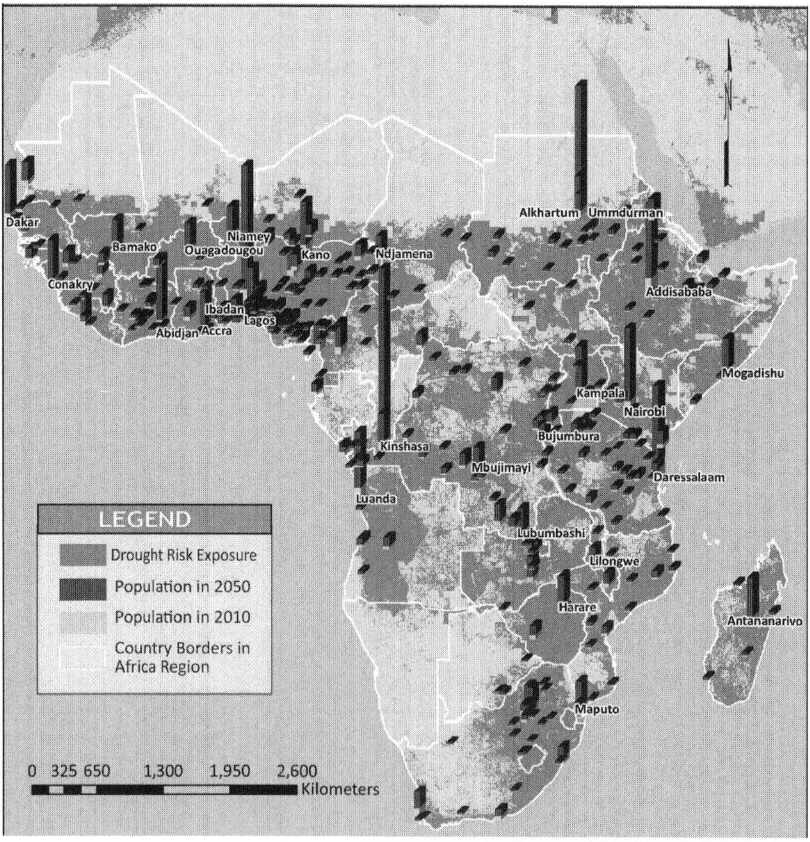

Source: Map produced by Africa Spatial Services Helpdesk, based on World Bank, 2012b.

throughout Africa are vulnerable to droughts and floods. For example, a large proportion of Kenya routinely suffers from both floods and droughts, often in the same year, and stream flow in the Niger River and its tributary, the Benue River, have varied greatly since 1900.

There is not enough water storage infrastructure (including both small check-dams and larger multipurpose storage systems) to compensate for hydrological variation in almost all areas. In Africa, storage capacity averages about 200 cubic meters per person per year, compared to about 6,000 cubic meters per person per year in North America and 2,400 cubic meters per person per year in China. Most countries in Africa for which data are available have less than 500 cubic meters storage per capita and many are significantly below this amount. At the same time a country such as Kenya has about the same (low) availability of fresh water per capita as Tunisia, which in turn has several times as much storage (Figure 1.12). In Africa existing storage infrastructure is generally inadequate to reduce flood peaks and augment low-season flows in highly variable river systems (World Bank, 2011a).

Floods affect the highest number of people in Africa after famine and epidemics; droughts and floods account for 80 percent of loss of life and 70 percent of economic losses linked to natural hazards (World Bank, 2012b). Recent floods in Accra, Dakar, and Maputo are a grim example of the serious impact of floods on African cities. In the last few years, many countries have suffered from repeated floods, with up to 1.7 million people affected and economic losses of up to US$330 million from a single flooding event. In West Africa alone, floods affect an average of 500,000 people per year, and this number is growing. Between 2008 and 2010, major floods in Benin, Burkina Faso, the Central African Republic, Madagascar, Namibia, Senegal, and Togo caused more than US$1 billion in damages and losses, and affected more than 2 billion people (World Bank, 2012b). In addition, the incidence and intensity of natural disasters in the region is rising (see Figure 1.13): the number of natural disasters in Africa has grown from about 20 per year in the 1980s and 1990s to about 60 per year in the 2000s (World Bank, 2010c, based on EMDAT[2]), with a marked increase in the number of flood events.

Although disaster data is not disaggregated for urban and rural areas, urban areas are likely to suffer more deaths and economic losses. There is a strong link between high rates of urbanization and increased vulnerability to natural hazards (World Bank, 2010c). Low-income urban residents often suffer the most as they move into marginal land that is prone to flooding. In 2009, floods in Senegal caused US$56 million in damages and

Figure 1.12   Water Storage in Africa (m³ per Capita)

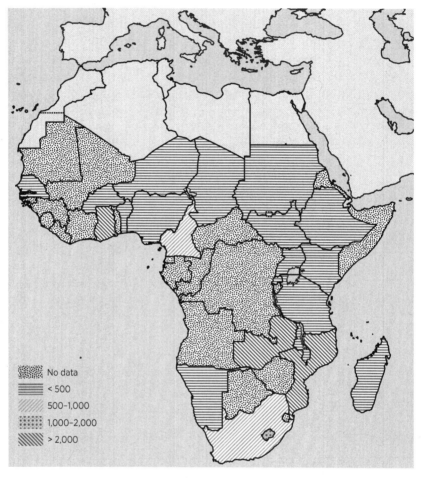

Source: Map produced by Africa Spatial Services Helpdesk, based on World Bank, 2011a.
Note: m³ = cubic meters.

another US$48 million in economic losses. Dakar, the largest city in the country, suffered most of the damage, with more than 360,000 people affected out of a total of 485,000 in the country as a whole (World Bank, 2012).

Recurrent urban disasters can also cause significant economic damage on an annual basis. Recurrent floods in Bangui, the largest city of the Central African Republic, left many people homeless and caused an aver-

Figure 1.13   Increased Frequency and Impact of Reported Disasters in Africa

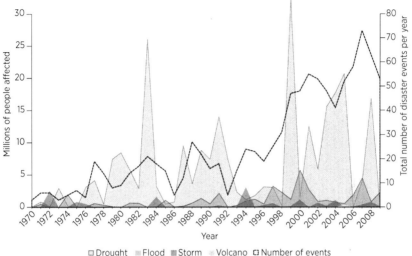

Source: World Bank, 2010c, based on EMDAT Emergency Events database 2010.

age US$7 million in damages and losses per year. In 2009, urban floods in the southwestern neighborhoods of Bangui left 14,500 people homeless. Over 40 percent of victims were under 14 years old, and 57 percent were female (World Bank, 2012). Diseases such as malaria, diarrhea, and other water-borne illnesses followed the floods, affecting lives and livelihoods, but the specific effect varies from region to region and the exact effect on African cities is difficult to predict.

Uncertainty might be the biggest threat to cities from climate change. Projected changes in precipitation up to the year 2075 vary widely between the different global circulation models, and none are fine-scaled enough to project change to the climate of specific cities. However, nearly all climate change projections signal greater chances of severe drought in Africa. Lower precipitation is projected to threaten food production and increase the risk of disease. Increases in sea level, cyclones, storm surges, and wind intensity will be experienced in many countries, particularly those on the coast (Dasgupta et al., 2009). In most places, in particular around the equator, climate change will increase climate variation. Given an uncertain future, plans for water sources, storage, and drainage will need to be flexible and adaptive to respond to a range of future conditions.

Secondary Cities are Equally at Risk but Even Less Equipped to Manage Complexity

Over the next 15 years, 38 percent of urban demographic growth is predicted to occur in cities of under 1 million people. While 35 percent of urban residents in Africa currently live in one of 42 cities with more than 1 million inhabitants, a significant proportion of urban dwellers live in intermediate cities (100,000 to 1 million inhabitants), secondary cities (50,000 to 100,000 inhabitants), and peri-urban areas (see Table 1.4). Cities under 1 million will grow by 38 percent by 2025; they have borne the bulk of the overall urban growth rate for the past decade (59 percent of growth from 2005 to 2010) and are projected to continue to grow rapidly (28 percent of growth from 2010 to 2025). For example, Nakuru, Kenya, and Dire Dawa, Ethiopia, grew at 16.6 percent and 7.8 percent, respectively, between 1990 and 2006 (Standard Bank, 2011).

The problems of secondary cities must be addressed as today's secondary cities might become tomorrow's megacities. The number of cities with populations of more than 1 million is projected to almost double from 42 in 2010 to 80 in 2025 (see Table 1.4). Thirty-one of Africa's current secondary cities will turn into cities with over 1 million residents over the next 15 years. The institutional, technological, and investment decisions those cities make today will impact their ability to cope with these new challenges.

There has been a tendency to focus investments in water and sanitation in capital cities. National utilities tend to privilege capital cities, leaving secondary cities underfunded, understaffed, and sometimes without functioning facilities altogether. Important regional disparities persist in rural access to drinking water, with sizeable gaps between the best and least served. Public expenditure often goes to where it is most easily spent instead of where it is most urgently needed, and often to where the politically powerful reside (van Ginneken et al., 2012).

High rates of population growth; large vulnerability to pollution; more competition for surface and groundwater sources; and less financial, managerial, and political capital to address the issues make secondary cities even more vulnerable to water-related challenges. The case of the Ugandan city of Masindi (Eckart et al., 2011) highlights the fragility of high-growth secondary cities with a single water supply source. Urban expansion combined with high economic growth (linked with the recent discovery of oil) will exacerbate water quality issues in the lake supplying all of Masindi's water. Under current management practice, water quality

Table 1.4 Africa's Urban Population, Number of Cities, and Percent of Urban Population

Parameter	Megacities (>10 million)	Very large cities (5–10 million)	Large cities (1–5 million)	Intermediate cities (500,000–1 million)	Fewer than 500,000	Total
Number of cities, 2005	0	2	37	33	n.a.	72+
Number of cities, 2010	1	1	40	44	n.a.	86+
Projected number of cities, 2025	2	7	71	71	n.a.	151+
Population, 2005 ('000)	0	15,625	68,843	22,143	141,795	248,407
Population, 2010 ('000)	10,788	8,415	85,592	30,783	162,823	298,402
Projected population, 2025 ('000)	33,392	45,129	153,957	47,142	225,931	505,550
% of urban population, 2005	0	6	28	9	57	100
% of urban population, 2010	4	3	29	10	55	100
Projected % of urban population, 2025	7	9	30	9	45	100

Source: UNDESA, 2012.
Note: n.a. = not applicable.

is bound to deteriorate drastically. As the town encroaches upon the lake's catchment, increased erosion will lead to the siltation of the lake, which will be further deteriorated by increased discharge of untreated wastewater from the city's growing population and increased water abstraction. It is in the interest of all stakeholders (including the city's industries) to preserve the lake's water quantity and quality by incorporating water into urban planning and industrial development plans.

Solving the Urban Water Challenge Is Essential to Achieve Growth and to Reduce Poverty

Urbanization is driving Africa's economic growth. Africa's urban population growth since 1960 has led to a concentration of population around major cities. Though urbanization is not uniform across the African continent and its causes are contested (Potts, 2012), urban population will exceed rural population in the next two decades. Concentration of production and income is even more pronounced than concentration of population (World Bank, 2011a). It is estimated that by 2025, 18 African cities (including Cairo, Cape Town, Johannesburg, Lagos, and Luanda) will control combined spending power of US$1.3 trillion, each with a GDP of over US$100 billion (McKinsey, 2011).

In most African countries, particularly the lower-income countries, insufficient infrastructure is a major constraint to doing business, and is found to depress firm productivity by about 40 percent. For most countries, the negative impact of deficient infrastructure is at least as large as that associated with corruption, crime, financial markets, and red tape (AICD, 2011). In general, adequate supply of electricity has the biggest impact on productivity, but transport, water, and sanitation are close behind. Furthermore, in several countries hydropower is a major source of electricity.

Water is central to Africa's development prospects, just as it has been the source of many of its past woes. It is clear that additional investments in water resources will be needed if Africa is to meet its needs for economical electric power; reliable supplies of water for irrigated agriculture, household consumption, and sanitation; and flood and flow control. It is equally clear that inadequate development and poor management of water have contributed to the droughts and floods that have devastated livelihoods, sparked resource-based conflicts, and undermined growth in Africa.

Water scarcity impacts negatively on production and incomes in cities due to extra time spent to get water, extra costs of abstraction (for example, deeper boreholes), and production lost due to disruptions to energy supplies for hydropower (see Table 1.5). In a water crisis with water rationing, the urban poor are disproportionately affected as they have no storage. Climate change and variability are likely to give rise to more climate extremes. The cost of inaction might be high.

Table 1.5   Estimated Cost of Droughts and Floods in Kenya

Attribute	Effect	Associated cost	Estimated cost (US$ million)
Drought	Crop loss	Crop loss	241
	Livestock loss	Livestock deaths, veterinary costs, reduced livestock production, conflict management	138
	Forest fires	Forest destruction and damage	—
	Fishery damage	Reduced aquaculture production	—
	Reduced hydropower generation	Increased generation cost and need to import substitute	642
	Reduced industrial production	Loss of production	1,400
	Impaired water supply	Increased water collection time, time loss due to conflict management meetings, cost of water vendor in Nairobi	508
Total droughts			2,929
Floods	Damage to infrastructure	Damaged water systems, road networks, communications, and buildings	822
	Public health hazard	Treatment costs	56
	Crop loss	Crop loss and reduced production	—
Total floods			878

Source: World Bank, 2005.
Note: Estimated costs due to floods are for 1997–98 events. Estimated costs due to droughts are for 1998–2000 events. — = not available.

Lack of Data Complicates Finding Solutions

Water resource data are deficient. There are few gauging stations for precipitation and surface-water levels; existing stations are often not functional. There are even less data on groundwater (MacDonald et al., 2011), and the impacts of climate variability and anthropogenic factors on watersheds are not well known. There are significant gaps in climate data; hydrometeorological networks are poor; and agencies often do not share data. These data deficiencies complicate accurate analysis and solutions.

The knowledge partnerships and collaboration between the scientific and development communities on climate change and water resources should be improved. This is essential to ensure that the latest scientific advances are reflected in development assistance and scientific questions explored are shaped by development needs. It is important that stakeholders at all levels become more aware of the specifics of climate-smart development planning.

Data on water supply and sanitation are poor, but better than other water subsectors. Despite significant efforts by the Joint Monitoring Program of the World Health Organization and the United Nations Children's Fund to systematically track data on access to water services, data quality is not always reliable. Systematic information and data about suppliers' characteristics and institutional environments are poor when they exist. Often, even the well-performing service providers are unrecognized outside their immediate environments, and lessons learned are not widely shared. The Africa Infrastructure Country Diagnostic (AICD) has made a limited effort to use a specially designed questionnaire on institutional environment, governance structure, and technical and financial performance to collect data covering 51 utilities in 23 countries.[3] Utility data are generally more useful to analyze water service issues within a city, but other than IBNET, few comprehensive, clean, datasets exist.

This study found that data on water supply, sanitation, flood management, solid waste, and water resources were even scarcer for cities. Some of the existing databases draw on household surveys, which might differentiate between urban and rural areas, but few report data at the city level.

The Current Way in Which We View Urban Water Systems Might Hinder Our Ability to Respond to Future Challenges

The challenge of servicing more people with scarcer water resources requires that we critically reappraise our current perspective on urban water management. Water demand is growing due to population growth and rising incomes. Supply is shrinking due to competing water users, deteriorating water quality, and overexploitation. And uncertainty about future conditions is becoming more acute because of climate change and shifting economies. We need to reconsider water use practices and develop strategies that can respond to all these challenges simultaneously.

It is no longer sufficient to build more water storage or harness more surface water without considering long-term sustainability, the larger watershed, or how wastewater can best be returned to the water system. It is no longer satisfactory to build better drainage to reduce dangerous flooding without making sure that drains are not clogged with solid waste; nor is it appropriate to ignore the sanitation needs of growing urban populations. It has become more difficult to plan for the long term when future conditions are uncertain. Management strategies must be flexible enough to accommodate multiple possible outcomes.

Water managers will need to broaden their field of vision to incorporate a wider perspective, and other institutions will need to incorporate water services in their long-term strategies. No single approach is likely to solve the potential water crisis for African cities. Decision makers will need to acknowledge the interrelatedness of challenges and evaluate the multiple pathways toward a solution.

Notes

1. For more information on the financial health of the utilities, see forthcoming city dashboards. http://water.worldbank.org/AfricaIUWM.
2. EMDAT is the Emergency Events Database maintained by the WHO Collaborating Centre for Research on the Epidemiology of Disasters (CRED) at the Universite Catholique Louvain, Belgium.
3. For more information about AICD, go to http://www.infrastructureafrica.org/.

CHAPTER 2

An Integrated Perspective for Urban Water Management

Integrated urban water management (IUWM) seeks to develop efficient, flexible urban water systems by adopting a holistic view of all components of the urban water cycle (water supply, sanitation, and stormwater management) in the context of the wider watershed.

The urban water shortages that are projected to get worse over the next century will require integrating solutions across scales (household, neighborhood, city, catchment, and transboundary), domains (economic, social, and environmental), and institutions (government, private sector, and civil society). IUWM is an adaptive approach in which decisions— reached by consultation with all stakeholders—are part of a long-term vision (Howe et al., 2011). It seeks to provide sustainable solutions that can respond to the increasing uncertainty about future conditions created by climate change and rapid growth (Khatri and Vairavamoorthy, 2007). The rapidly expanding cities of Africa are particularly suited to IUWM solutions because new infrastructure and management frameworks can be designed from the start using IUWM principles.

IUWM has a History of Knowledge and Good Practice

In response to the urbanization challenges, water professionals, city leaders, academics, and the World Bank have developed knowledge and practice on IUWM. This work has drawn on many sources, but has been particularly inspired by the Sustainable Water Management Improves Tomorrow's Cities Health (SWITCH) project, funded by the European Union (EU); work by the World Bank's Latin America and Caribbean Region Water Beam, the International Water Association Cities of the Future program; and work done at the United Nations Educational, Scientific and Cultural Organization under the auspices of the UNESCO-International Hydrological Programme (UNESCO-IHP) and the UNESCO Institute of Water Education (UNESCO-IHE).

The EU-funded SWITCH project,[1] which ran from 2006 to 2011, focused on the learning and the development of institutional and practical guidelines with respect to city planning, stakeholder participation, water supply, stormwater, wastewater, and decision-support tools. In each of 12 case studies across four continents, a specially created learning alliance provided a knowledge and decision-making platform for key stakeholders to collaborate on the definition and formulation of the strategic urban plan.

The World Bank has developed a series of projects integrating urban water services, urban development, drainage, and source protection; they were inspired by work with clients in Latin America and the Caribbean over a number of years. Based on a number of case studies (São Paulo and Recife, Brazil; Medellin, Colombia; and Mexico City and Monterrey, Mexico) the region has developed a conceptual framework for IUWM, which emphasizes the process of engagement. This framework is currently being tested in Tegucigalpa, Honduras, where it has led to the establishment of a stakeholder forum including institutions and civil society organizations developing an IUWM investment strategy.

The IWA Cities of the Future program focuses on water security for the world's cities and how the design of cities—and the water management, treatment, and delivery systems that serve them—could be harmonized and reengineered to minimize the use of scarce natural resources and increase the coverage of water and sanitation in lower- and middle-income countries. As one of the IWA's key programs, it has benefitted a number of events in support of stakeholder engagement, knowledge exchange, and knowledge development among water professionals.

UNESCO-IHP and the Institute of Water Education have both devoted programs committed to carrying out research, education, and capacity-building activities in the area of urban water management. UNESCO-IHP's Urban Water Management Program has published academic work on topics relevant to sustainable urban water management (for example, model simulation for urban groundwater management, and urban water management in arid and semiarid areas) as well as providing capacity-building support on key urban water issues. The UNESCO Institute of Water Education in Delft has a specific research theme focusing on developing research and solutions based on several key concepts of urban water management. Many graduates from this program work for large water utilities, regulators, or other public authorities throughout Africa.

The Urban Water Cycle Is One System

It is important to understand and articulate the relationship between the various components of the urban water system (water supply, wastewater, and stormwater) and to manage them as a single system. System components have a number of positive and negative interactions.

- Negative interactions include the impact of poor sanitation on the water quality of potential water sources, both surface and ground (Lee and Schwab, 2005; Tucci et al., 2009); and cross-contamination that takes place between leaky sewers, foul water bodies, and drinking-water supply pipes, which is particularly a problem with intermittent supply (Vairavamoorthy et al., 2007).
- Positive interactions include opportunities for considering a portfolio of water sources, reuse, recycling, and cascading use of water (GWP, 2010; Mitchell, 2004).

Analysis at different scales exposes different opportunities. Analysis at the household scale exposes opportunities for rainwater harvesting and greywater recycling (Batchelor et al., 2011); analysis at the neighborhood scale exposes opportunities for local surface water/groundwater use and wastewater recycling using natural systems (Bieker et al., 2010); and analysis at the city scale exposes interactions with road infrastructure and settlement structures and receiving water resources.

Box 2.1

Integration of Water Resource Management, Water Supply, and Sanitation: Polokwane, South Africa

Polokwane, the capital of Limpopo province in South Africa, was awarded Blue Drop status by the National Department of Water Affairs (DWAF) because of its recent achievements in water resource management and water supply management. Blue Drop Certification is an incentive-based regulation introduced by DWAF in 2008 to encourage excellent management of drinking water. Polokwane's reward is significant, considering that the city's dry climate requires water imports, and that rapid population growth and the demands of an expanding local economy have placed severe stresses on the system. Water sources in the region are precarious: natural inflows are low and dams were not planned for the emerging demand. The Polokwane Municipality Water Safety Plan includes safety plans for catchment areas, treatment plants, and the distribution system. Over the past few years, the strategy has emphasized building capacity to strengthen the coordination of water use and supply; a drought management plan, including increased use of recycled wastewater; demand management by expanding water metering and volumetric monitoring programs, including the introduction of pre-paid metering as well as a pressure reduction system to reduce water leakage; and a price structure in which the price of water increases with increased water usage, rewarding lower usage while also ensuring basic access for poorer households.

Challenges remain substantial, but the combination of national incentives and technical support, as well as concerted efforts to link water resource management and water supply, have made considerable progress possible.

Source: Bloch, 2012.

The Urban Water Cycle Is Closely Linked to the Watershed

The city depends on and impacts the wider watershed. Integrated water resources management applied to the watershed should consider urban issues. At the catchment scale, upstream changes in land use patterns and deforestation might alter the local hydrological cycle, necessitating watershed protection plans and water allocation strategies (Anderson and Iyaduri, 2003; Gleick et al., 2011). Measures at this scale might be crucial for a city's access to sufficient water of adequate quality as well as for flood protection. Conversely, the city impacts downstream users

Box 2.2

Watershed Management and Water Supply: Payment for Ecosystem Services in Heredia, Costa Rica

The province of Heredia in Costa Rica is naturally endowed with rich water resources. The Virilla River Watershed has an approximate surface area of 10,000 hectares and approximately 34 percent of the region is covered by forest. Surface and groundwater sources are abundant in the catchment, with 18 wells and 14 natural springs supplying more than 15 million cubic meters per year to the province.

Despite a lack of treatment infrastructure, the province of Heredia is the only one in Costa Rica to have 100 percent access to water supply for its 200,000 inhabitants. In 2000, the local water supply company (Empresa de Servicios Públicos de Heredia) designed a plan for payments for environmental services aimed at providing access to safe drinking water by protecting strategic forest areas for the recharge of surface and groundwater sources in the catchment. In this plan, forest conservation was seen as an investment and regulation against changes in land use patterns was approved to protect the sources of water supply for the province. The water company put in place new economic instruments in the form of added fees to the water bill (around 3 percent of the monthly water bill) so that end users could directly contribute to the protection of designated strategic water resource areas. The funds collected through this scheme are used to compensate landowners in the designated areas for the control of changes in land use. Over the last 10 years, the program has protected more than 1,100 hectares of forest within the catchment.

Source: Barrantes and Gamez, 2007.

through the quality and quantity of the water discharged from sewers and treatment plants.

Water Should Be Managed across Institutions

Institutionally, in most countries the political responsibility for water resource management is held by national governments, while local institutions or dedicated national supply companies are tasked with water supply and sanitation services. This distinction between national resource management and regional and local service delivery has brought a necessary level of specialization. However, in most African countries, it has also resulted in poorly coordinated planning for water supply management and poorly defined roles and responsibilities. In water-scarce and financially stressed African cities, the ramifications of this lack of coordination and conflation of roles have been a lack of strategic planning and accountability. Steeped in an assumption of abundance in the former restricted-growth urban environments of the colonial era, the planning, construction, and management by the public sector—at relatively low cost—of centralized city water supply schemes were believed sufficient to secure water availability. In these past urban environments, this centralized approach adequately served the requirements of an urban elite, and to some extent of the poorer communities (Bloch, 2012).

In modern African cities, however, informal settlements have grown rapidly, and many people live outside the formally planned urban system. Water supply systems and the institutions that manage them face significant challenges to adapt to the greater fluidity this requires. In today's African city, centralized systems do not reach substantial parts of the urban populations who live in growing peri-urban settlements. The IUWM paradigm has provided some models for the broader, more integrated approaches required in this dynamic environment (Bloch, 2012).

Good governance is a critical component to any water management agenda. Institutions need to be accountable and clear about their roles. The criteria for priorities should be made clear. Local governments, regulatory authorities, utilities, and so on should receive (financial) resource allocations that correspond to the responsibilities conferred upon them by central authorities.

Sustainable finance is necessary, including adequate cost recovery from tariffs or taxes. Financially, most African city governments or water companies are not fiscally strong or self-sufficient, and for many the transfers of tax revenues they receive from higher tiers of government are not adequate or sufficiently predictable to compensate for insufficient tariff revenues. The result has been underinvestment, inadequate maintenance, and deterioration of assets. In the absence of clear incentives to deliver responsive services, revenue management to enhance local and/or utility financial sustainability has also been weak.

Good governance policies and strong finance must be accompanied by the tools and capacities with which to make the policies work (Butterworth et al., 2011). This will require the development of appropriate legislative, planning, implementation, and management tools, as well as the introduction of mechanisms to manage increased revenue for water resource development activities. In part, this is an issue of providing better professional skills and financial resources to address critical areas such as integrated water resource planning and management, as well as the operation and maintenance of water-related infrastructure and services. Cities need strategic investment to meet access targets and long-term sustainable outcomes. For the water sector, such a strategic approach requires linking management and planning of water resources and supply to broader urban planning, management, and financing.

It is important that water professionals understand and appreciate the significant role of urban planning in potentially supporting or constraining the optimization of their water systems. This requires close coordination, early in the development stage, between planners and water professionals (Binney et al., 2010; Brown et al., 2008). A clustered approach to urban development facilitates the development of decentralized systems, which foster the reuse of treated wastewater (Bieker et al., 2010). A survey of African water utilities revealed that the attitude among African water professionals about the integration of urban planning and sectoral perspectives is ahead of current practice (see Chapter 3 of this book).

Box 2.3

Integration across Legislative and Strategic Frameworks: South African Integrated Development Plans

Legislative reform in post-apartheid South Africa sought to decentralize government activities. The introduction of integrated development plans (IDPs) represented a shift in municipal governance toward more management- and performance-oriented criteria. The 1998 White Paper on Local Government positioned the IDP as an integral part of the legislative reform as well as an essential instrument in the planning and management of local government activities. In 2000, the Municipal Services Act specified the minimum contents of the IDP as

- a vision for the long-term development of a municipality
- an assessment of the current level of servicing, and of economic and social development in a municipality

(continued on next page)

Box 2.3 *(continued)*

- the municipal council's development priorities and objectives for its elected term
- the local council's development strategies (which must be aligned with any national or provincial plans)
- a spatial development framework (which must include guidelines for a land use management system)
- operational strategies
- sectoral plans required by other legislation (for example, water plans, transport plans, waste management plans, disaster management plans, and housing strategies)
- a financial plan
- a set of key performance indicators and performance targets.

Although initially positioned as an instrument of local planning and coordination, the IDP is now linked in an intergovernmental planning system, and includes instruments such as the national government's Medium-Term Strategic Framework and Provincial Growth and Development Strategies.

South Africa's effort to develop an integrated development framework highlights the importance of integration across legislative, strategic, and detailed frameworks. By adopting a management approach, the stated objectives are linked to human- and financial-resource allocation and provide a framework for implementation and operation.

Source: Harrison, 2006.

Box 2.4

A Holistic Approach to Urban Planning: Indore's Slum Network Project

Indore's Slum Network Project (SNP) in India is a project that adopts a holistic approach to urban improvement in which slums are seen as an integral part of the city. Instead of ignoring and denying the reality of slums, it used slums as

(continued on next page)

Box 2.4 *(continued)*

urban nets to upgrade the whole city in an integrated way. The SNP worked at two broad levels: slums and the city. At the level of slums, it substantially upgraded the quality of life through engineering innovations, notably the creation of individual infrastructure and improvement in the overall slum environment. At the level of the city, instead of upgrading slums on a slum-by-slum basis, it considered the entire network of slums so that it became an opportunity for augmenting city infrastructure. This is because watercourses, which are major locations of slum settlements, also represent the most efficient lines for infrastructure provision.

New infrastructure provided in the individual slums was linked to that of other slums and to the existing city systems to bring about significant improvements to the city as a whole. The SNP generated economies of scale: the cost of underground sewerage and centralized treatment under the Slum Networking approach was Rs 1,500 (US$44) per slum family for the on-site provisions and Rs 1,000 (US$30) for the off-site collection and treatment. This total cost of Rs 2,500 (US$74) was the same as that of a shared twin pit latrine (developed by the United Nations Development Programme) but the advantages are considerably greater (that is, all families have individual facilities and a much cleaner living environment).

Source: Diacon, 1997.

All Players Should Be Part of the Process

Critical to the success of IUWM is the early and continuous integration of all stakeholders—including the public—in the planning, decision-making, and implementation process. Stakeholder and public participation can improve the scope of decision making and can help to create long-term and widely acceptable solutions. It is important to ensure that decisions are soundly based on shared knowledge, experience, and evidence; that decisions are influenced by the views and experience of those affected by them; that innovative and creative options are considered; and that new arrangements are workable and acceptable to the public (European Commission, 2002).

Stakeholder engagement can break down barriers to information sharing and learning and speed up the identification, development, and uptake of solutions related to urban water management (Butterworth et al., 2011). To be successful, engagement should ensure that expectations about the process are well framed and understood by all players.

Box 2.5

Public Participation in Allocating Scarce Water: The Eastern Australian Experience

In the mid-1990s Australia embarked on a program of water allocation reform, with increased public participation where new initiatives were proposed. Since then, severe drought conditions have prevailed in Eastern Australia for nearly 10 years, with rainfall falling by 30 percent from historic averages in key agricultural regions. Despite these dramatic reductions in water availability, overall agricultural contributions to the economy have been maintained. The pain of losses to farmers has been cushioned through the buy-back program, whereby irrigators in rural areas could sell their water rights and essentially either move out of agriculture or revert to rainfed agriculture.

Public acceptance of losses in farm income through the prolonged droughts was achieved in part through credible information communicated effectively to all stakeholders. A Community Reference Panel was the main means of public participation in this process. Capacity building of participants, independent scientific support, and access to data were some of the most critical factors promoting effective public participation.

Because the public had the opportunity to participate in and influence decision making in water allocation, some potential legal conflicts were avoided, although recent (2011) developments indicate that underlying conflicts still exist. In response to the proposal by the River Basin Authority of a Basin Plan for the Murray Darling, irrigators have argued that the control and limitation of river flows for consumptive uses and the establishment of environmental flows limit the potential of economic growth for river-dependent industries. On the other hand, the proposed amendments to the Basin Plan by the state of South Australia argue for new environmental and economic models to be used in the calculations for the reduction of consumptive extractions. At the same time, environmentalists claim that the environmental flows are not sufficient to sustain key natural assets and ecosystem functions in the Basin. Public participation can improve decision making, but it is not a panacea.

Sources: Martin and Puddy, 2012; Tan, 2006.

Water Should Be Fit for Purpose

Supplying water that is fit for purpose—that is, matching water quality to its intended use—will change the requirements of water demand and reduce water abstraction. The application of this principle exposes alternative sources of water that can be safely used for different purposes and can help address the growing gap between water demand and supply caused by the competition for water sources by different users (GWP, 2010; Maheepala et al., 2010; Vairavamoorthy et al., 2008). Some examples of cascading and recycling include greywater reuse for toilet flushing or gardening and nonpotable water for nonprocess industrial demand (Allen et al., 2010; Morel and Diener, 2006; Vairavamoorthy et al., 2009). By avoiding the need for the highest level of treatment for some applications, water can be reused, reducing gross water abstraction and water treatment costs (Foo, 2007; Muller, 2010).

Box 2.6

Cascading Use of Water for Urban Agriculture: Accra, Ghana

Irrigated urban vegetable production in Accra provides up to 90 percent of the vegetable needs of the city (Tettey-Lowor, 2009). Most of the agricultural sites are located on valley bottoms along streams and drainage systems and use raw wastewater as the main source for irrigation. The research project SWITCH developed institutional guidelines and piloted a low-cost treatment system to facilitate the safe reuse of wastewater for irrigation while minimizing health risks. A demonstration project was established at the Dzorwulu-Roman Ridge site, which covers an area of 8.3 hectares in Accra.

Source: Reymond et al., 2009.

Box 2.7

Water Fit for Industrial Use: Durban, South Africa

The concept of water fit for purpose has been implemented in the city of Durban, South Africa, to respond to a conflict between water demand for domestic use and economic development under conditions of water scarcity.

(continued on next page)

Box 2.7 (continued)

Figure B2.7.1   Dual Benefits of Water Fit for Purpose: Reduced Consumption of Fresh Water and Reduced Wastewater Discharge

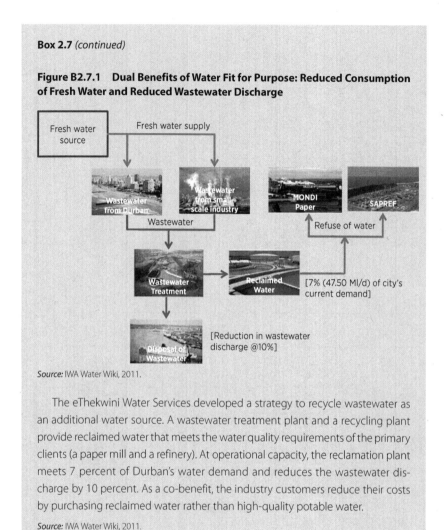

Source: IWA Water Wiki, 2011.

The eThekwini Water Services developed a strategy to recycle wastewater as an additional water source. A wastewater treatment plant and a recycling plant provide reclaimed water that meets the water quality requirements of the primary clients (a paper mill and a refinery). At operational capacity, the reclamation plant meets 7 percent of Durban's water demand and reduces the wastewater discharge by 10 percent. As a co-benefit, the industry customers reduce their costs by purchasing reclaimed water rather than high-quality potable water.

Source: IWA Water Wiki, 2011.

Diverse Sources Provide Better Water Security

Given shrinking water supplies, rising demand and cost, and uncertainty about the future, it is necessary to explore diverse and flexible options for water sources. A broader range of water sources increases the reliability and security of the water supply (Alcamo et al., 2008; Gleick, 2009). Groundwater is the most obvious source to supplement surface water, but other options such as stormwater, greywater, and blackwater should also be considered. For example, following a decade of work, the new Nairobi Master Plan considered a large range of options, and groundwater was introduced as a major and systematic water source for the first time in Nairobi's history (Hirji, 2012).

By combining the concepts of water fit for purpose and security through diversity, all potential water sources can be modeled to maximize end use and system efficiency. This approach can reduce fresh water use and costs and may improve environmental outcomes (Donkor and Wolde, 2011; GWP, 2010; Sharma and Vairavamoorthy, 2009).[2]

Box 2.8

Combining Water Fit for Purpose and Security through Diversity: Windhoek, Namibia

With annual rainfall of only about 370 millimeters, high surface evaporation rates, and a distance of 750 kilometers to the closest perennial river, Windhoek faces severe challenges in securing its water supply. All potable water resources within a radius of 500 kilometers have been fully exploited. And the city is growing rapidly.

Driven by these pressures, Windhoek now relies on four main sources of water: surface water from dams; groundwater from 50 municipal production boreholes; reclaimed water from the New Goreangab Water Reclamation Plant (NGWRP); and reclaimed water from the Old Goreangab Water Reclamation Plant (OGWRP). While the NGWRP reclaimed water contributes to the potable water consumption of the city, the reclaimed water from OGWRP is used to irrigate parks, golf courses, and cemeteries. Windhoek is one of the few systems in the world that recycles treated wastewater for drinking water.

Figure B2.8.1   Water Sources for Windhoek, Namibia

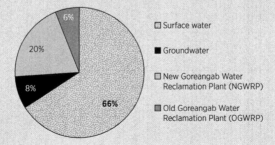

Sources: Lahnsteiner et al., 2007; Van der Merwe, 2000.

Urban Groundwater: Sustaining Water Security and Increasing Water Treatment Potential

For some cities, groundwater represents a strategic resource to sustain baseline water supply for their population. It can also be used to maintain water demand during drought or to increase security of supply affected by reduced river flow. Given the expected urban population growth rates and in view of some climate change scenarios, groundwater expansion is considered as one of the preferred responses in areas of Africa where suitable aquifers are present (Foster et al., 2010b).

Urban water management can make use of the hydrogeological characteristics of groundwater to improve water supply. Aquifers have the potential to be used as seasonal water storage through groundwater recharge processes and water reuse schemes, which sometimes incorporate this type of solution. Different types of aquifer recharge techniques allow the infiltration of treated sewage effluent to facilitate nutrient and pathogen removal. The recovery of such water after pumping enables its use for water supply purposes after treatment (Dillon et al., 2009).

Groundwater abstraction in urban areas is generally done with little conjunctive use of surface and groundwater (Foster et al., 2006). In rapidly expanding cities, conjunctive use of surface water, groundwater storage, and abstraction can complement urban water supply and add security and flexibility in case of seasonal resource variation. Coordinating management responsibilities that are currently divided between local and national administrations, and informing practitioners of the benefits of rational, conjunctive surface-groundwater development, can improve resource use and delivery of urban water services (Foster et al., 2010a).

Groundwater abstraction in cities in Africa tends to be informally organized. In Sub-Saharan Africa only a few large urban water utilities—for example, Abidjan, Bamako, Dodoma, and Lusaka—use groundwater as a permanent source of supply (Foster et al., 2010b). However, privately owned boreholes and wells for direct water collection (or reticulation to standposts) have widely become the fastest growing source of urban water. According to some estimates, 24 percent of urban water supply is collected from waterwells, which represent the fastest growing source and serve an additional 1.5 percent per year of the urban population (Tuinhof and Heederik, 2003). In some areas that lack or have a poor municipal water supply and/or high water prices, groundwater is privately abstracted, resulting in a mushrooming of private in situ well construction. Enforcement of regulation of private wells in urban areas is difficult and may result in over-abstraction of the aquifer (Foster et al., 2010b).

Localized groundwater abstraction in urban areas presents significant groundwater quality challenges that need to be addressed when planning for current and future water supplies. Wastewater infiltration from poorly maintained latrines can pollute aquifers, hence groundwater protection and improved wastewater management and sanitation are connected issues (Foster et al., 2006). Additionally, groundwater quality concerns are more acute in coastal areas where the lack of control of aquifer pumping can cause salinity problems due to seawater intrusion.

Box 2.9

An Innovative Approach Leads to the Discovery of the Kimbiji Aquifer, a Potentially Important Water Supply Source for Dar es Salaam, Tanzania

The Kimbiji Aquifer System, a previously unknown aquifer, was discovered in 2006 as part of Dar es Salaam (Tanzania) Future Water Source Masterplan Development, under the World Bank–funded Dar es Salaam Water Supply and Sanitation Project. Twenty-six supply options (including on-stream and off-stream dams, interbasin transfers, shallow and deep groundwater, and desalination) were reviewed but only two were further investigated: the deep Kimbiji Aquifer and Kidunda Dam.

The groundwater study concluded that the Kimbiji Aquifer System is an important potential source of water to cover Dar es Salaam water demand through 2030. It is estimated to cover an area of 10,000 square kilometers and have a storage volume of approximately 1 million liters (or megaliter—Ml). Average annual recharge rate is estimated to be about 1,000 Ml/year—an enormous potential water source compared to the city's estimated additional 2030 water demand of around 200 Ml/day.

The existing water supply for the city comes from the Ruvu River, a surface water source to the north. The Kimbiji Aquifer is located south of the city. With adequate management and protection, this large natural reservoir will remain a strategic water source for the rapidly growing area. Conjunctive use and management of surface and groundwater can offer the Dar es Salaam Water Supply and Sewerage Authority the flexibility to effectively respond to hydrological variability during periods of drought. Moreover, the Kimbiji Aquifer (as a naturally buffered system) offers resilience from the impacts of climate change on the city's water supply.

Sources: Hirji, 2012; Ruden, 2007.

(continued on next page)

Box 2.9 *(continued)*

Figure B2.9.1   Existing Urban Water Supply and Future Groundwater Source for Dar es Salaam, Tanzania

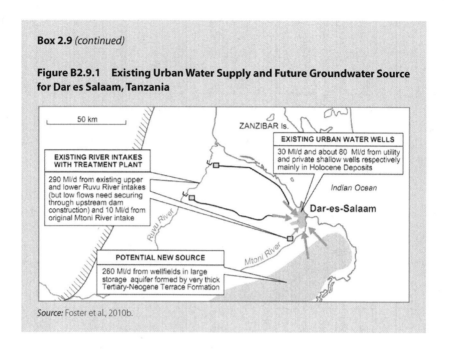

Source: Foster et al., 2010b.

Innovative Technologies Can Play a Role

Technological innovations can help respond to the challenge of servicing more people with water and wastewater services under conditions of diminishing supply. Innovative treatment technologies might enhance recycling of wastewater and ensure that water can be used multiple times. Energy-efficient treatment options have been developed around natural systems (such as constructed wetlands and soil aquifer treatment), providing reliable treatment of multiple contaminants in a single system. Flexible technologies, such as small-scale, decentralized stormwater measures, can be optimized over time. Established technologies, such as membrane technologies, have recently undergone developments that drastically reduce their production costs, allowing small-scale applications to become cost-effective (Peter-Varbanets et al., 2009).

Treatment technologies have traditionally been viewed as linear systems, where water enters and leaves the system as a single stream of specific quality. A perspective to treatment based on innovative technologies is emerging where waters of different qualities are received and produced within a single system (Bieker et al., 2010; Cornell et al., 2011; Otterpohl et al., 2003). In addition, recent advances have generated efficient treatment options, such as membrane bio-reactors, and relatively simple technologies, such as soil aquifer treatment (Essandoh et al., 2009) and decentralized wastewater treatment systems (BORDA, 2012). The low-cost and low-energy requirements of these technologies are well suited to conditions in developing countries, and open up opportunities for communities to consider reuse, recycling, and cascading use.

In many cases, innovative technologies are being hindered by old regulations such as building codes and health codes. During a workshop in Nairobi with stakeholders, representatives of the Nairobi City Council raised the need to revise building codes to permit such technologies as urban rainwater harvesting and greywater separation (ICLEI, 2012a). In many cases national codes, such as health codes that often date to the colonial era, will have to be revised.

Box 2.10

Decentralized Wastewater Treatment System as an Effective Technology to Improve Sanitation: Trapeang Sab Commune, Cambodia

In the Trapeang Sab Commune, the main town was rapidly urbanizing and its traditional sanitation practices were no longer effective. The untreated wastewater being released in increasing volumes in the commune was becoming a hindrance to development because of groundwater pollution and public health issues.

The decentralized wastewater treatment system (DEWATS) was implemented to serve 250 households and small businesses with a capacity of 100 cubic meters per day. The project had a total project cost of US$50,200. The system consists of a primary settling unit, an anaerobic baffled reactor, an anaerobic filter, and a discharge pipe. An operator was contracted by the Commune Council to be responsible for general operations and maintenance of the DEWATS.

The treated effluent is in compliance with the Cambodia Ministry of Environment's regulations for wastewater effluent discharged into public waters and sewers (chemical oxygen demand < 100 milligrams per liter and biological oxygen demand < 80 milligrams per liter). The Trapeang Sab DEWATS discharges effluent with a chemical oxygen demand of 94 milligrams per liter and a biological oxygen demand of 46 milligrams per liter. Total coliform has not been measured, but similar technologies such as waste stabilization ponds and constructed wetlands report total coliform removal of 97 percent.

Source: IWA Water Wiki, 2012.

Wastewater Might Be Valuable

There is great potential in urban water systems for water, energy, and nutrient recovery. In particular, wastewater is often grossly undervalued as a potential resource. By employing innovative technologies, water, calorific energy, biogas, and nutrients can be reclaimed from different water and waste streams and reused locally as shown in Figure 2.1 (Bieker et al., 2010; Cornell et al., 2011; Otterpohl et al., 2003). The so-called water machine would also enable the reclamation of water of different qualities that are fit for different purposes.

Figure 2.1   Resource Recovery from Wastewater: The "Water Machine" Concept

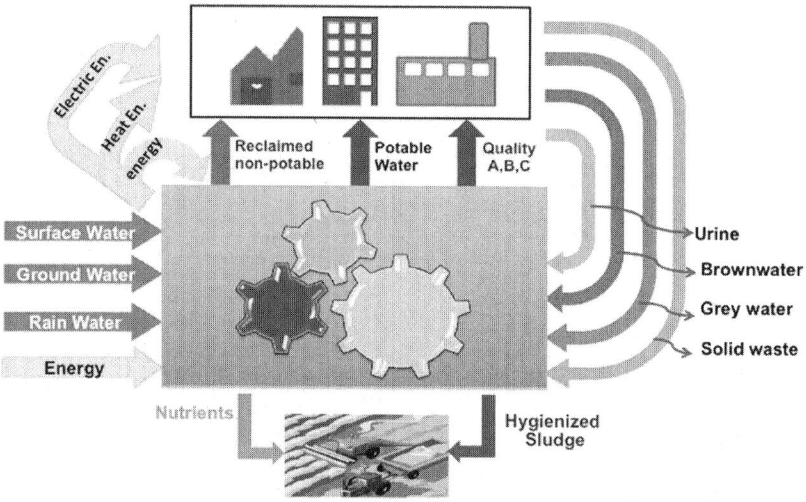

Source: World Bank, based on Bieker et al., 2010; Cornell et al., 2011; Otterpohl et al., 2003.

A perspective to treatment is emerging that aims to maximize the benefits reaped from every drop of water. Recent advances have generated technologies for simple, low-cost solutions, allowing the "water machine" concept to be applied in developing countries. Wastewater treatment and reuse in agriculture can provide benefits to farmers in conserving freshwater resources, improving soil integrity, and improving economic efficiency. In addition, wastewater has the potential to provide renewable energy and nutrients and will convert current liabilities (energy required for wastewater treatment) into assets (energy from wastewater treatment). Such a perspective raises the possibility of addressing the sanitation challenge in African cities as an opportunity rather than a burden (Howe et al., 2011).

Box 2.11

Wastewater as a Source of Energy: Naivasha, Kenya

A lavatory, wastewater treatment, and biogas generation facility started operation in 2008 adjacent to the Naivasha Bus Park in Naivasha (a small town 90 kilometers northwest of Nairobi). It consists of five toilet cubicles, two showers, and one urinal with the wastewater from the facility being treated and used for biogas and water generation. The biogas generation project (including the water kiosk) is operated by the Water Services Trust Fund and had a total investment cost of approximately US$50,000.

The facility served about 300 visitors per day in 2009 and provides biogas for cooking for a nearby kiosk. The facility is managed by the local water service provider, who contracted a local community-based organization to operate the toilet on a pay-per-use basis.

Figure B2.11.1   Lavatory and Wastewater Treatment Plant with Installed Biogas Generation Facility in Naivasha, Kenya

Source: Rieck and Onyango, 2010.

To generate energy from the wastewater, a biogas plant with a capacity of 54 cubic meters was constructed to anaerobically pretreat the wastewater from the toilets, showers, and wash basins, lowering the organic pollution load. Treated effluent is discharged to an existing public sewer and the accumulated sludge is removed once a year and can be used as a fertilizer.

The biogas is piped (through 1.5 centimeter galvanized iron pipe) to a nearby café where it is used for cooking. A water trap chamber is installed next to the biogas plant to collect condensed water in the pipe.

Source: Rieck and Onyango, 2010.

Adaptive Systems Work Best to Cope with Uncertainty

Water management must take into account that the future is inherently uncertain. It is important to recognize that there is uncertainty about many future conditions including population distributions, economic growth, and climate change. A flexible strategy that can adapt over time to changing requirements is critical (Vairavamoorthy et al., 2008). The principles of IUWM outlined previously foster the use of flexible technologies and approaches to planning that can respond to the uncertainty about the future paths of expanding African cities.

A more modular, decentralized approach to urban water management and a clustered growth approach to urban development are particularly important components in planning for an uncertain future (Bieker et al.,

---

Box 2.12

Flexible Design of Decentralized Wastewater Treatment and Reuse Systems: Xi'an, China

In the newly developed housing area outside Xi'an in northwestern China, an expansive green space was considered necessary both to increase the real estate's commercial value and to improve living conditions. Because the water demand for gardening is high, treated wastewater was used for watering to mitigate urban water shortages (Wang et al., 2008). In the city of Xi'an, there were two options for wastewater reuse: a supply of reclaimed water from treated wastewater through a centralized pipe system; and the use of decentralized wastewater treatment systems (DEWATS) for onsite reuse. DEWATS were cost efficient, and they could be implemented more quickly than the centralized system. The decentralized system could also be implemented incrementally, which provided the flexibility to trace the urban growth trajectory and to avoid up-front investment.

A pilot project was implemented that included six residential buildings for 400 people. The wastewater management system includes a dual-piping sewer system for separate collection of blackwater and greywater. The greywater is treated by a process combining enhanced primary treatment with ozone-enhanced flotation that included chemical coagulation, biodegradation, particle pelletization, and separation in one unit. The treated greywater is used to replenish an artificial pond with a water surface area of 6,500 square meters (0.5 meters deep) that maintains a green belt that covers an area of 6,400 square meters.

Source: Wang et al., 2008.

2010). Modular diversity exponentially increases the number of possible configurations that can be achieved for urban water systems from a given set of inputs. This approach generates options for urban water systems that have internal degrees of freedom, which allow their performance to be optimized over time (Ashley et al., 2007; Eckart et al., 2010). The clustered approach to urban development optimizes the adaptive capacity of the emerging urban space by allowing infrastructure provision to be staged in a way that traces the urban growth trajectory more carefully. In addition, this ability to stage infrastructure provision over time means that emerging clusters can implement the latest innovations when they become available. All these options have value, an important point that is missed in traditional economic analysis. It is important for the assessment of adaptive systems to use analyses that recognize the value of options.

Notes

1. See http://www.switchurban.eu.
2. See example for Australia in Eckart et al., 2011, where the city of Melbourne has committed itself to total water cycle management. The approach considers all components of the urban water cycle with the aims of reducing reliance on vulnerable water supplies, improving water quality, and adapting to climate change.

CHAPTER 3

Assessing Water Management Challenges and Capacities in African Cities

African cities face a myriad of challenges in providing water to their residents. The integrated urban water management (IUWM) options presented in Chapter 2 of this book can be part of a solution, but applying them will take time, money, knowledge, and above all the institutional capacity to make decisions that cross-cut sectors. Policy making across sectors will require cooperation and dialogue between responsible administrators and all stakeholders. Some African cities are well placed to implement changes, and others will need to build capacity to work more effectively. The nature of the challenges also varies widely depending on geographic, demographic, and economic conditions. This book attempts to unravel some of this complexity by conducting a survey of urban administrators; closely examining the available data on 31 representative African cities to create an index of water management challenges and capacities and a database of key indicators; creating future urban extent maps for these cities; and using climate change projections at the basin scale to project possible climate change effects on the 31 cities.

As with other city databases, the quality of available city-level data used for this analysis was far from optimal. The gaps and limitations of the data available from public sources and the lack of regular monitoring represent serious hindrances to the understanding of current and future needs and to the ability to plan for meeting these needs. There is not enough data available for almost all areas relevant to urban water management—particularly for informal settlements—including data on hydrometeorology, water resources, water services, and coping strategies, as well as information on related factors such as population and land use. One of the primary recommendations of this book (presented in Chapter 5) is to improve research and data about African cities. By presenting the data that are currently available, supplemented by new data sets generated for this book, we hope to stimulate two discussions: one on data needs, and another on the substance of the relevance of an IUWM approach for specific cities.

Knowledge and Attitudes to Urban Water Management Are More Evolved than Its Practice in Africa

Knowledge, attitudes, and practices (KAP) in relation to urban water management is crucial for the ability to act. Together with the African Water Association and the United Cities and Local Governments of Africa, we conducted a KAP survey among municipal and utility leaders (see Appendix 1 for methodology). The questionnaire was responded to by 13 of 39 municipalities (33 percent) and 24 of 80 utilities (30 percent).

Utility decision makers believe that a wide range of issues need to be considered as part of an urban water management plan. In addition to traditional water and sanitation issues, utilities identified issues related to flood and drought risk, services to the poor, links to urban planning, and expected population growth (see Figure 3.1).

However, current plans have a more restricted coverage. Only two out of three utilities in large African cities responding to the questionnaire have an approved water master plan. Within the approved plans, less than half are known to include consideration of urban drainage, solid waste management, drought and flood contingency plans, rainwater harvesting, and urban land zoning.

Municipal leaders agree that their future plans should include a wide range of issues related to urban water management. More than 80 percent of leaders from cities think that their future plans should include issues such as rainwater harvesting, and drought and flood contingency plans.

However, municipalities have more encompassing current plans than utilities. The results of the survey also show that municipalities include in their current urban plans a wider array of issues than water utilities.

IUWM approaches are intended to widen the range of issues from an early planning stage. This seems to partly match the needs recognized in

Figure 3.1   Issues Included in Current Plans, and Issues African Leaders Think Should Be Included in Future Plans

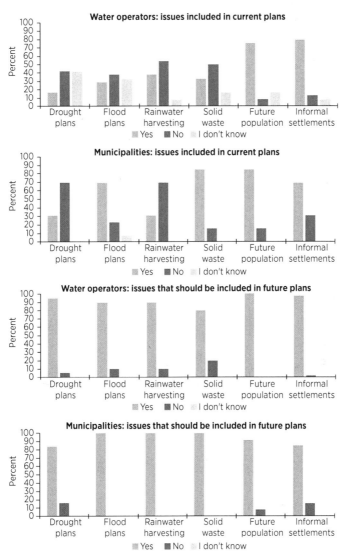

the survey. While cities and utilities generally think that the range of issues should be broadened for key IUWM issues, such as wastewater reuse, only about half of the cities believe this to be an issue to be included. This might indicate that these cities face no scarcity issues or other reasons to consider wastewater reuse, or it might reflect a lack of awareness. Although most cities and utilities include informal settlements in their current plans, more than 20 percent of the cities in the sample moderately disagree with the inclusion of water supply to informal settlements in future urban plans.

There is a wider range of actors involved in overall urban water management planning than in the water management planning done by a utility (see Figure 3.2). The current level of citizen and end user involvement is low (20 percent of responses) and advocacy will be needed to increase end user involvement.

City leaders and water operators agree that emphasizing the importance of institutional structures and political will should help achieve better urban water management. City and utility leaders have also stressed the necessity of creating more institutional cooperation and developing institutional frameworks to help meet future planning challenges. However, these institutional arrangements have to be specific and fit in with the local and national governance structures. In some cases, decentralization practices or regulation laws might affect urban water management practices. In Dakar, for example, the municipality finds that incorporating additional water network maintenance responsibilities into the city's urban plan is difficult due to decentralization laws and the division of responsibilities between the national and local government.

Figure 3.2   Involved Parties in the Consultation Process of Urban Water Management: From the Municipality (Left) and Utility (Right) Viewpoints

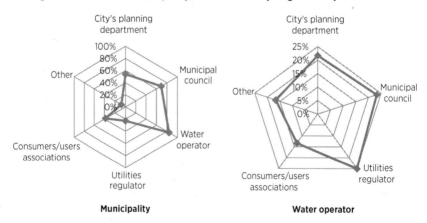

Source: World Bank.

Reducing Complexity to Two Dimensions: IUWM Capacities and Challenges Index

We have collected publicly available information for 31 cities to create an index that measures the challenges faced by cities and the capacity of cities to meet these challenges through IUWM. These cities have been selected to represent the biggest (more than 2 million population) and fastest growing (at least 1 million and more than 3 percent growth) cities in Africa, complemented by a few major cities where the World Bank has active water management programs—for example, Cotonou and Lilongwe (see Figure 3.3). These data have been used to create an IUWM challenges and capacities index and a database of relevant information.[1]

Figure 3.3   Cities in Africa Selected for the Diagnostic

Indices have a long tradition in development work. While an indicator-based index is not a scientific approach to predict IUWM challenges and capacities (Kraay and Tawara, 2010), such indices have been found to generate a dialogue about causes of success and promote monitoring systems. The index presented here is intended to serve this purpose (see Appendixes 2 and 3 for methodology).

In this two-dimensional index,[2] we consider cities have a larger challenge relevant for an IUWM approach when:

- **Urbanization challenges** are strong due to high growth in population and a large share of informal population
- **Solid waste management challenges** are strong reflecting low levels of solid waste collection and disposal in controlled sites
- **Water supply services** are characterized by low levels of water sold per capita and limited coverage with improved water supply
- **Sanitation services** are characterized by low levels of wastewater treatment, high levels of water-borne diseases, and limited coverage with improved sanitation
- **Flood hazards and vulnerability are higher** as represented by a larger number of flooding events
- **Water resources availability** in the basin is less.

We consider cities have a higher capacity to deal with such challenges when:

- **Country policies and institutions are stronger**, as evaluated by the World Bank
- Cities have more **economic strength** (using national data as proxy)
- **Water-related institutions are stronger**, as represented by a regulatory setup that conforms more closely to "standard international" recommendations and has targets for pro-poor services
- **Water utility governance** is stronger (using financial indicators as proxy).

Most African cities face substantial water management challenges and have limited capacity, but of these cities some are relatively more challenged and some have relatively more capacity (see Figure 3.4). Cities such as Blantyre, Lilongwe, and Luanda are the most challenged, while cities such as Cape Town, Durban, Johannesburg, Dakar, and Douala are less challenged. Not surprisingly, we find that the three South African

Figure 3.4   Urban Water Management Challenges versus Institutional and Economic Capacities

Index 0–1.00

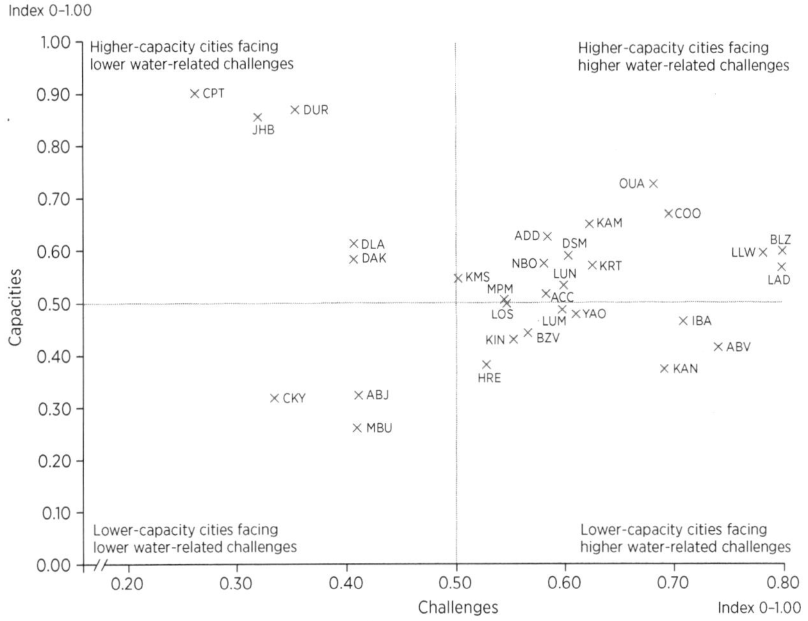

Source: World Bank.

Note: City abbreviations: ABJ, Abidjan, Côte d'Ivoire; ABV, Abuja, Nigeria; ACC, Accra, Ghana; ADD, Addis Ababa, Ethiopia; BLZ, Blantyre, Malawi; BZV, Brazzaville, Republic of Congo; CKY, Conakry, Guinea; COO, Cotonou, Benin; CPT, Cape Town, South Africa; DAK, Dakar, Senegal; DLA, Douala, Cameroon; DSM, Dar es Salaam, Tanzania; DUR, Durban, South Africa; HRE, Harare, Zimbabwe; IBA, Ibadan, Nigeria; JHB, Johannesburg, South Africa; KAM, Kampala, Uganda; KAN, Kano, Nigeria; KIN, Kinshasa, Democratic Republic of Congo; KMS, Kumasi, Ghana; KRT, Khartoum, Sudan; LAD, Luanda, Angola; LLW, Lilongwe, Malawi; LOS, Lagos, Nigeria; LUM, Lubumbashi, Democratic Republic of Congo; LUN, Lusaka, Zambia; MBU, Mbuji-Mayi, Democratic Republic of Congo; MPM, Maputo, Mozambique; NBO, Nairobi, Kenya; OUA, Ouagadougou, Burkina Faso; YAO, Yaounde, Cameroon.

Note on methodology: The figure presents an index that categorizes cities in two dimensions: water-related challenges and institutional and economic capacities. For each dimension, a number of variables were identified, for which indicators were then selected. For the water-related challenges dimension, indicators were selected for the following variables: urbanization challenges, solid waste management, water supply services, sanitation services, flood hazards, and water resources availability. For the institutional and economic capacities dimension, indicators were selected for the following variables: country policies and institutions, economic strength, water-related institutions, and water utility governance. Indicators were normalized, thus unit values vary from 0 to 1. Indicators were assigned equal weights and aggregated for each dimension. For further details, see Appendixes 2 and 3.

cities in the sample have relatively large capacities, while cities in the Democratic Republic of Congo have less capacity to deal with their challenges. It is possibly more surprising that the three South African cities also come out as having relatively less challenges. This reflects that challenges are measured as yet unmet challenges. For example, a city with a high rate of water supply and sanitation (WSS) coverage is deemed to have a smaller challenge for the future than a city with a low rate of WSS coverage, even if achieving that high rate of coverage might have been very challenging in the past.

Cities that face relatively strong challenges and have relatively high capacity are candidates for early consideration of IUWM. Cities with higher challenges are likely to have greater need of an emphasis on water fit for purpose, security through a diversity of sources, and wastewater as a valuable resource. At the same time, linking aspects of planning across sectors and spatial scales and involving all stakeholders will demand more institutional capacity. For each specific case, an assessment of the value of each approach should be made.

Although the challenges of secondary cities might be at least as great as those for large and capital cities, unfortunately not enough data was available to allow us to make a similar overview for secondary cities.

You Cannot Manage What You Do Not Measure: A City Dashboard as a Starting Point for Dialogue

Urban water management challenges are complex, and capacities at the city level are hard to isolate. City-level information is typically available in city-specific documents and only to a limited extent in global or regional databases.[3] Furthermore, even when information is available, there are no agreed standards (such as International Organization for Standardization standards) for reporting, so seemingly similar data might be defined differently. Finally, much of the required information is only available at the national or regional level (for example, economic production and income data) or for urban areas (for example, Joint Monitoring Program data and other household survey–based data). Such information is difficult to compare across cities. To make information available that is comparable and city based as far as possible, we have developed a dashboard with pertinent information for each of the 31 large African cities (for methodology, see Appendixes 2 and 3). This provides a starting point for a review of complex challenges and capacities, and in the longer run a starting point for a cities database for African cities, similar to the Global City Indicators Program.[4]

The dashboard illustrates the water management challenges, as well as indicators for capacity for good water management practices, for each city relative to other cities (see Figure 3.5). Indicators for challenges focus on water scarcity, urban population growth, water and sanitation services access, flood risk, and solid waste management at the city level. Indicators

Figure 3.5   Comparative Indicators for Urban Water Challenges for 31 African Cities

Urbanization Challenge   ⬤ More desirable   ⬤ Less desirable

Well below average	Below average	Average	Above average	Well above average
Harare	Maputo	Ibadan	Lusaka	Yaoundé
	Kano	Douala	Lagos	Kumasi
	Johannesburg	Addis Ababa	Ouagadougou	Luanda
	Cape Town	Accra	Kinshasa	Abuja
	Durban	Conakry	Lilongwe	Dar es Salaam
	Khartoum	Nairobi		
	Cotonou	Kampala		
	Abidjan	Lubumbashi		
	Dakar	Mbuji-Mayi		
	Blantyre	Brazzaville		

Solid Waste Management   ⬤ More desirable   ⬤ Less desirable

Well above average	Above average	Average	Below average	Well below average
Maputo	Nairobi	Ibadan	Kano	Mbuji-Mayi
Johannesburg		Khartoum	Cotonou	
Cape Town		Lusaka	Blantyre	
Durban		Harare		
Douala		Yaoundé		
Conakry		Abidjan		
		Kumasi		
		Lagos		
		Kampala		
		Ouagadougou		
		Dar es Salaam		

No data—Addis Ababa, Accra, Dakar, Luanda, Kinshasa, Lubumbashi, Brazzaville, Lilongwe, Abuja

(continued on next page)

Figure 3.5 *(continued)*

Water Resources Availability   ◐ More desirable ● Less desirable

Well above average	Above average	Average	Below average	Well below average
Douala Yaoundé Conakry Kinshasa Brazzaville	Addis Ababa Kumasi Lubumbashi Abuja	Maputo Ibadan Kano Cape Town Durban Lusaka Harare Cotonou Abidjan Accra Nairobi Lagos Dakar Kampala Ouagadougou Mbuji-Mayi Blantyre Lilongwe Dar es Salaam	Johannesburg Khartoum Luanda	

Water Supply Service   ◐ More desirable ● Less desirable

Well above average	Above average	Average	Below average	Well below average
Cape Town Abidjan Dakar	Johannesburg Durban Khartoum Cotonou Addis Ababa Kumasi Conakry Nairobi Kampala Ouagadougou Lubumbashi Blantyre Lilongwe Dar es Salaam	Lusaka Harare Yaoundé Lagos Kinshasa Mbuji-Mayi	Maputo Ibadan Kano Douala Accra Luanda Brazzaville Abuja	

(continued on next page)

Figure 3.5 *(continued)*

Sanitation Service

More desirable ● Less desirable

Well above average	Above average	Average	Below average	Well below average
Johannesburg	Maputo	Ibadan	Cotonou	
Cape Town	Dakar	Kano	Luanda	
Durban	Dar es Salaam	Khartoum	Ouagadougou	
Kumasi		Lusaka	Lubumbashi	
Nairobi		Harare	Brazzaville	
Lagos		Douala	Blantyre	
Kampala		Yaoundé	Lilongwe	
		Abidjan		
		Addis Ababa		
		Accra		
		Conakry		
		Kinshasa		

No data—Mbuji-Mayi, Abuja

Flood Hazard in River Basin

More desirable ● Less desirable

Well below average	Below average	Average	Above average	Well above average
	Johannesburg	Maputo		Kano
	Lusaka	Ibadan		Khartoum
	Harare	Cape Town		Cotonou
	Douala	Durban		Nairobi
	Yaoundé	Addis Ababa		Kampala
	Abidjan	Conakry		Ouagadougou
	Accra	Lagos		Lubumbashi
	Kumasi	Dakar		Blantyre
	Mbuji-Mayi	Luanda		Lilongwe
		Kinshasa		Abuja
		Brazzaville		
		Dar es Salaam		

Source: World Bank.
Note: The tables show the different degrees of desirability for a selection of variables illustrating either capacities or challenges affecting IUWM in 31 cities in Africa. Each column contains the overall position above or below the average for a combination of different indicators (see Appendixes 2 and 3). Depending on whether the indicators reflect challenges or capacities associated with IUWM, it will be more or less desirable to have a value below or above the average for the 31 cities. A color gradation has been used to help clarify the degree of desirability for each variable.

for capacity focus on governance, institutional setup and planning, and economic development. The limitations in the data gathered highlight the need for larger and broader based efforts to generate, collate, and present comparable data at the city level. Despite data issues and the disparities among cities a few conclusions stand out.

The need for a safe and continuous water supply for growing populations meets the reality of old and poorly functioning infrastructures in many cities in Africa. Nonrevenue water exceeds 40 percent for 18 of the 31 cities,[5] indicating that systems are old and poorly maintained. Forty percent of the utilities have an operating ratio inferior to 100 percent,[6] meaning that their revenues do not cover their operating costs; and for two-thirds of them (68 percent), the operating ratio is less than our benchmark of 130 percent, meaning that they are struggling to cover their costs. Of the 31 cities surveyed, only five cities have a sustainable rate of bill collection (defined as a 95 percent collection ratio).[7] In many cities, ensuring good governance and adequate financing will be critical to upgrading old infrastructure and extending service to new areas.

Population and water demand are growing very rapidly in some cities. The population in 17 of the 31 cities is growing at an annual rate of more than 3.7 percent. This is equivalent to a doubling time of 19 years. Of these 17 cities Abuja, Kumasi, Luanda, Ouagadougou, and Yaoundé exhibit growth rates of more than 5.3 percent per year. A growth of 5.3 percent is equivalent to a doubling time of 13 years. If income grows as well, water demand might double in 10 years or less. This exacerbates the challenges of water management and highlights the need to explore diverse water sources, including reused wastewater, to ensure that water is fit for purpose and to exploit innovative technologies.

Certain cities are in areas that are naturally freshwater scarce (for example, Johannesburg) whereas other cities are in areas that have abundant natural water availability (for example, Kinshasa). Cities in arid or semiarid regions might abstract water from a distance (for example, Johannesburg and Nairobi); pump from artisan groundwater deposits (for example, Dar es Salaam); or, for coastal cities, exploit seawater that is abundant but costly to use. In all these cases, the engineering challenges and the cost of securing water are likely to be high. There are a few exceptions, such as Khartoum, of cities in arid regions located on major rivers.

Many cities have high population densities, and a large proportion of residents live in informal settlements. Of the 31 cities in this study, 14 have a population density of more than 8,000 inhabitants per square kilometer; and 21 have densities higher than densely populated cities such as Rio de Janeiro (with 5,900 inhabitants per square kilometer) or Beijing (with 4,200 inhabitants per square kilometer). In more than half (17) of the cities, between one-half and three-quarters of the population live in informal areas.

In 13 of the 31 cities, less than half the population has access to improved sanitation. This represents a serious social, health, and environmental challenge (Water and Sanitation Program, 2012). In addition, contamination from the informal areas can have a negative health affect for populations in richer parts of the city. In Indore, reducing this health threat was a major driver behind their slum upgrading program (see Chapter 2, Box 2.4). By managing the urban water cycle as a single system, the contamination of water sources by poor sanitation might be lessened.

The Spatial Dimensions of a Growing City Matter to Water Management

Rapid urbanization and its spatial dimensions are key drivers of several aspects of the urban water management challenge. However, traditionally, we know little about the location and size of the future development areas.

To fill the void, we created maps of past and future urban extent for the 31 selected cities based on satellite imagery and on a methodology for projection of future urban extent.[8] This work complements the groundbreaking research by the Lincoln Institute (Angel et al., 2010) that consists of historic maps for 120 cities globally, including 11 cities in Africa. In addition, using a simplified, cellular automata approach based on the Slope, Landuse, Urban Extent, Transportation and Hillshade (SLEUTH) model (Clarke et al., 1997), we developed another set of future extent maps for these 31 cities.[9]

Future urbanization is described through a four-step process:

1. Define suitability for future urbanization of the areas surrounding the existing city.
2. Exclude certain areas from urbanization (for example, water bodies, national parks, and so on).
3. Determine the size of the future area to be urbanized (in our case by the year 2025).
4. Allocate population growth to highest suitability areas first, then the next suitable, and so on.

The city of Abuja is growing rapidly (see Figure 3.6), and its spatial growth is likely to follow a starfish-like pattern, with roads as one of the facilitators of further urbanization. This growth pattern has two important characteristics for water management: it is difficult to predict as it will depend on such factors as road construction, and it will cause a centralized, piped network to become very long. In this case, the modular

Figure 3.6   Illustration of Future Urban Extent for a Mature City (Top) and for a Fast-Growing City (Bottom)

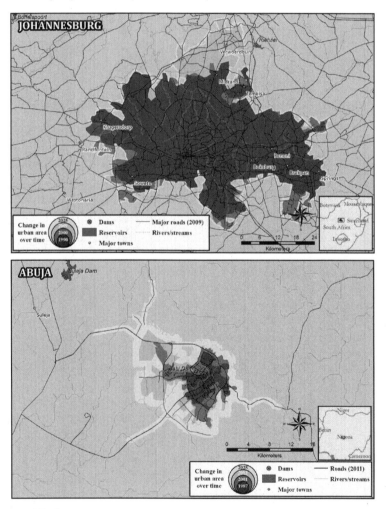

Source: World Bank.
Note: Maps available for download from the website: http://water.worldbank.org/AfricaUWM.

approach to growth, fostered by IUWM, might be more adaptive and suited to help cope with an uncertain growth pattern.

Coastal cities like Lagos or Luanda (see Figure 3.7) will face additional challenges related to urban growth. Future urban water management plans will not only have to consider water resources and supply but also address vulnerable storm surge and flood areas and the impact of future

Figure 3.7   Illustrations of Future Urban Extent for Two Coastal Cities (Top Panels) in Areas Vulnerable to Flooding from Rising Sea Level (Bottom Panels)

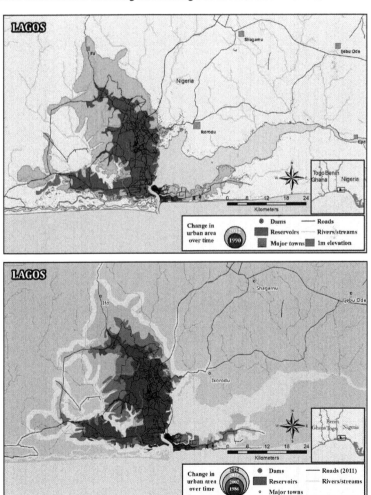

(continued on next page)

Figure 3.7 *(continued)*

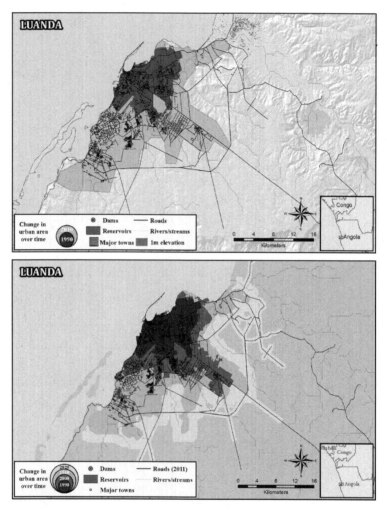

Source: World Bank.
Note: Maps available for download from the Website: http://water.worldbank.org/AfricaIUWM.

sea-level rise on coastal settlements, including informal settlements (see Figure 3.7 bottom).

The created urban extent maps illustrate the potential to spatially enable water management planning. Better decisions can be made if water management planning is closely linked to urban planning, and if detailed consideration is given to not only how much water demand will increase in the future, but also the likely spatial dimensions of this demand, and how this relates to the spatial distribution of current and potential future supplies.

Climate Change Will Have an Impact on Urban Water Management

While little information is available about future climates at the city level, some information about future hydrology at the catchment level is available.[10] The basin is a relevant intermediary scale to provide information about the catchments upon which cities depend for water supply. In Table 3.1 we present an analysis of future hydrology at catchment level in accordance with World Bank methodology (Strzepek et al., 2011). The analysis utilizes five hydrology indicators (measures of changes in mean annual runoff, slow onset floods, droughts, storage, and groundwater) to assess the potential impact of climate change on water resources. The table illustrates the likelihood of lower (higher) values of these indicators for the city-relevant catchment.[11]

Unfortunately, for most cities in Africa and for most of their indicators, there is little agreement among the climate models. To a large extent this reflects the limited ability of the climate models to model weather in Africa. This again reflects the paucity of historic climate data for Africa and the difficulties that the models have in modeling both the oscillations such as the El Niño Southern Oscillation and the expected frequency and impact of convective storms.

Table 3.1 Cities, Water, and Climate Change in 2050: An Indicator Approach to Understanding the Risk for 31 Cities

Hydrology indicator	Lower with high confidence	Lower with medium confidence	Little agreement among models	Higher with medium confidence	Higher with high confidence
Mean annual runoff	MPM, CPT, DUR	ADD, DAK, JHB	LAD, COO, OUA, YAO, DLA, BZV, KIN, LUM, MBU, ABJ, ACC, KMS, CKY, NBO, BLZ, LLW, ABV, IBA, KAN, LOS, KRT, KAM, LUN, HRE	DSM	—
q10 (flood indicator)[a]	MPM, DAK, CPT, DUR	ADD	LAD, COO, OUA, YAO, DLA, BZV, KIN, MBU, ABJ, ACC, KMS, CKY, NBO, BLZ, LLW, ABV, IBA, KAN, LOS, JHB, KRT, KAM, LUN, HRE	LUM, DSM	—
q90 (drought indicator)[b]	CPT, JHB	CKY, BLZ, MPM, DAK, DUR	LAD, COO, OUA, YAO, DLA, BZV, KIN, LUM, MBU, ABJ, ADD, ACC, KMS, LLW, ABV, IBA, KAN, LOS, KRT, KAM, LUN, HRE	NBO, DSM	—
Basin yield (storage)	NBO	LAD, ADD, DAK, JHB, KRT	COO, OUA, YAO, BZV, KIN, LUM, MBU, ABJ, ACC, KMS, CKY, BLZ, LLW, MPM, ABV, IBA, KAN, LOS, CPT, DUR, KAM, HRE	DLA, DSM	LUN
Base yield (groundwater)	CPT	ABJ, BLZ, MPM, DAK, DUR, JHB	LAD, COO, OUA, YAO, DLA, BZV, KIN, LUM, MBU, ADD, ACC, KMS, CKY, NBO, LLW, ABV, IBA, KAN, LOS, KRT, KAM, LUN, HRE	DSM	—

Sources: Data from the World Bank Climate Change Knowledge portal and Strzepek et al., 2011.

Note: Lower/higher with high confidence: 17 or more of the 19 climate models (90 percent) for emission scenarios A2 give this result (19 of the Intergovernmental Panel on Climate Change AR4 models provide results for the A2 emission scenario). Lower/higher with medium confidence: 13 to 16 of 19 climate models give this result (67 percent). Little agreement among models: between 7 and 12 of 19 climate models give the same sign of change (lower or higher).

[a] q10 is the flow that is exceeded 10 percent of the time. For q10 an increase in the value signifies an increase in the likelihood of a given high flow and therefore an indication of increased flood risk.

[b] q90 is the flow that is exceeded 90 percent of the time. For q90 a decrease in the value signifies an increase in the likelihood of a given low flow and therefore an indication of increased drought risk.

City abbreviations: ABJ, Abidjan, Côte d'Ivoire; ABV, Abuja, Nigeria; ACC, Accra, Ghana; ADD, Addis Ababa, Ethiopia; BLZ, Blantyre, Malawi; BZV, Brazzaville, Republic of Congo; CKY, Conakry, Guinea; COO, Cotonou, Benin; CPT, Cape Town, South Africa; DAK, Dakar, Senegal; DLA, Douala, Cameroon; DSM, Dar es Salaam, Tanzania; DUR, Durban, South Africa; HRE, Harare, Zimbabwe; IBA, Ibadan, Nigeria; JHB, Johannesburg, South Africa; KAM, Kampala, Uganda; KAN, Kano, Nigeria; KIN, Kinshasa, Democratic Republic of Congo; KMS, Kumasi, Ghana; KRT, Khartoum, Sudan; LAD, Luanda, Angola; LLW, Lilongwe, Malawi; LOS, Lagos, Nigeria; LUM, Lubumbashi, Democratic Republic of Congo; LUN, Lusaka, Zambia; MBU, Mbuji-Mayi, Democratic Republic of Congo; MPM, Maputo, Mozambique; NBO, Nairobi, Kenya; OUA, Ouagadougou, Burkina Faso; YAO, Yaoundé, Cameroon. — = not available.

Notes

1. For full report of the index see Naughton, Closas, and Jacobsen, (forthcoming) (http://water.worldbank.org/AfricaIUWM).

2. For a detailed methodology and a full list of indicators, see Appendix 3. Appendix 2 outlines the relevance of these variables for IUWM and gives a detailed methodology.

3. Global databases that provide city-level indicators include UN-Habitat and the United Nations Department of Economic and Social Affairs. However, for water and sanitation services indicators, confusion can arise from databases such as the International Benchmarking Network for Water and Sanitation Utilities, as the utilities surveyed can be national- or city-level, and the Joint Monitoring Program of the World Health Organization and the United Nations Children's Fund, which categorizes indicators in urban and rural categories, but does not differentiate between cities.

4. See the website for the Global City Indicators Program: http://www.cityindicators.org. For full details of the cities database see Naughton, Closas, and Jacobsen (forthcoming) (http://water.worldbank.org/AfricaIUWM).

5. Nonrevenue water (as per IBNET definition) is the difference between volume of water supplied and volume of water sold. This difference is expressed as a percentage of net water supplied.

6. Operating ratio (as per IBNET definition) is defined as total annual operating revenues/total annual operating costs.

7. Information on billing (collection ratio) is for one year only, but years reported vary per city. For the cities database, the last reported year is taken.

8. These maps will be available on http://water.worldbank.org/AfricaIUWM, in a forthcoming companion volume to this report.

9. See Appendix 4 for a detailed description of the methodology. For full details and all maps see Duncan, Blankespoor, and Engstrom (forthcoming) (http://water.worldbank.org/AfricaIUWM).

10. This information is available on the World Bank Climate Change Knowledge portal: http://sdwebx.worldbank.org/climateportal/index.cfm. To access the data click on a point on the climate portal map; for example: http://sdwebx.worldbank.org/climateportal/index.cfm?page=country_impacts_water&ThisRegion=Africa&ThisCcode=TZA.

11. For full details on climate change analysis see McCluskey, Duncan, Blankespoor, and Naughton (forthcoming) (http://water.worldbank.org/AfricaIUWM).

CHAPTER 4

In-Depth Analysis of Water Management Challenges in Selected Cities

City-specific circumstances will be critical in assessing whether and how an integrated urban water management (IUWM) approach would be relevant. A number of cities worldwide have adopted IUWM approaches, in Latin America in particular—for example, Belo Horizonte and São Paulo, Brazil; Cali, Medellin, and Bogotá, Colombia; and Monterey, Mexico (SWITCH, 2011). But it is not clear if all cities would benefit from such an approach. This study undertook intensive case studies of three African cities to identify potential IUWM strategies that would help public authorities deal with the challenges of water management.

Based on a call for potentially interested cities among World Bank task team leaders, three cities were selected as case studies to assess the benefits that IUWM might provide: Nairobi (Kenya) and Arua and Mbale (Uganda), complemented by a desk review in Douala (Cameroon). The selected cities include both medium- and large-size cities with different administrative traditions, and each has different challenges. Deliberately, the chosen cities have water management projects in an early phase (just before or just after World Bank approval), and the analysis under this economic and sector work could move into a practical implementation phase if there was interest from the city client. As will be described, city authorities expressed interest in concrete follow-up in each of the three cities selected as case studies.

Nairobi, Kenya: Dealing with the Gap between Supply and Demand

Table 4.1   Key Characteristics and Location of Nairobi, Kenya

Population (2009)	3,140,000
Estimated daytime population (2010)	5,000,000
Projected annual population growth	2.50–5.00%
Economic activity	Industrial, commercial
Water consumption per person served	n.a.
Utility water coverage	63%

Source: Eckart et al, 2012.
Note: n.a. = not available.

Nairobi presents a classic case of how the gap between water supply and demand might grow over time (see Chapter 1). Since 1985, the population of Nairobi has grown from approximately 1.2 million in 1985 to 3.2 million in 2010. During the same period, water demand grew slightly faster, from 203,000 cubic meters per day to 579,000 cubic meters per day (AWSB, 2012). In 2009, Nairobi experienced a crisis as water levels in the main reservoir became very low and water supply to the city had to be severely rationed.

The water crisis provided a strong impetus to change. Work on a new water master plan has been ongoing for some time and is expected to be finalized during the summer of 2012. An Agence Française de Développement funded project to reduce nonrevenue water, with a focus on water losses, has started. Ongoing efforts to enhance the bulk water storage and transfer infrastructure have been complemented by additional work on IUWM in Nairobi, prepared as a case study for this book (Eckart et al., 2012).

Nairobi faces major uncertainties in assessing the gap between future water demand and supply. The case study reviewed the population, income, and water consumption per capita projections. Even small changes to the assessment of the high- and low-growth scenarios for population and unit consumption result in a large range of possible demand in 20 years (see Figure 4.1). Other sources of uncertainty, including the impact of future climate variability and climate change, add to the degree of uncertainty about projected water supply and demand. This illustrates the need to implement adaptive systems that can cope with uncertainty as suggested by the principles of IUWM.

Figure 4.1   Estimated Range of Future Water Demand for Nairobi, Kenya, 2010 to 2035

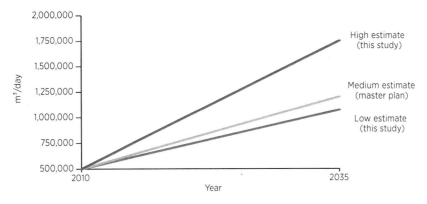

Source: World Bank, based on water master plan estimate from (AWSB, 2012).
Note: m³ = cubic meters.

Decentralization creates additional uncertainties about future conditions for bulk water supply to Nairobi. The new constitution of Kenya will result in a stronger role for lower levels of government by allocating to county governments the responsibility for public works and services, including water and sanitation. Water resources cross counties and regions, and, while they will remain a national resource, there will need to be agreement on specific management arrangements. For Nairobi, which imports most of its water from the Tana basin outside Nairobi county, such disagreements might cause uncertainty about the access to and the cost and reliability of these surface water resources.

IUWM is a potentially powerful approach to water security through diversification in Nairobi. As an adaptive system, IUWM options in Nairobi's future water system can provide water security within a much wider range of future water demand and supply scenarios and can help offset or defer bulky investments in conventional water resources. Even though each of the proposed options only provides a small gain individually, in combination they can provide a more significant contribution to the solution of the water resource challenge in Nairobi. The proposed IUWM options include water demand management, leakage management, stormwater harvesting, and greywater recycling. It is suggested that the options be implemented at the household, cluster, or city level depending on the policy scenario chosen by decision makers. Not all scenarios include all options.[1]

When the quality of water is matched with its intended purpose, there are more options for diversification. Figures 4.2 and 4.3 compare the

Figure 4.2   Staged Development of Water Resources for Nairobi, Kenya, 2010 to 2035

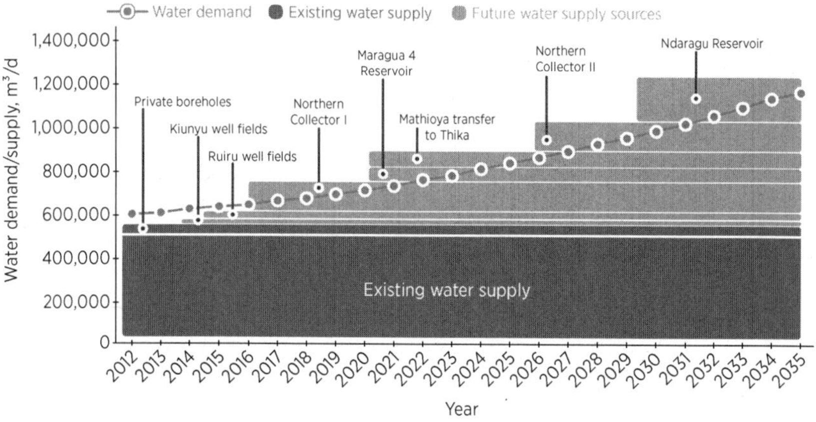

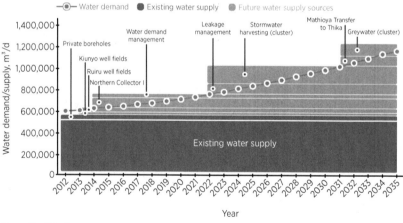

Source: World Bank, based on data from AWSB, 2012.
Note: m³/d = cubic meters per day.

Figure 4.3   Staged Development of Water Resources for Nairobi, Kenya, 2010 to 2035, for One Alternative IUWM Solution

Source: World Bank.
Note: The figure shows the years at which the different water sources need to be developed to meet the growing water demand for Nairobi. The volume of water supplies from each source has been determined based on meeting medium-term water demand projections. Some of the sources might need to be developed at the same time (for example, Northern Collector 1 and water demand management; leakage management and stormwater harvesting). m³/d = cubic meters per day.

most recent proposals from the draft water master plan (AWSB, 2012) with one of the scenarios from the IUWM systems approach that includes a number of additional sources of water, including stormwater and greywater. It should be noted that stormwater and greywater are not used directly for household use, but either used for nonpotable uses or recharging of groundwater (Eckart et al., 2012).

The IUWM options provide more resilience to unexpected outcomes. Figures 4.2 and 4.3 illustrate how consideration of additional sources of water may allow postponement of some water supply infrastructure. Alternatively, those same sources could function as a buffer against higher demand and/or lower water supply than anticipated in the planning forecast for the Feasibility Study and Master Plan for Nairobi (AWSB, 2012).

By modeling the urban water cycle as one system, we find that solutions are available to address the water gap in Nairobi at reasonable cost. Cost schedules were developed for a wide variety of water sources (see Annex 2 of Eckart et al., 2012). These illustrate a large variation in costs depending on specific circumstances, for example, whether solutions are implemented at household or at cluster level. As an illustration, we provide the cost calculation for the staged development, IUWM scenario 2; see Figure 4.4 (Eckart et al., 2012).

Figure 4.4   Water Resources and Unit Costs for One Alternative IUWM Solution

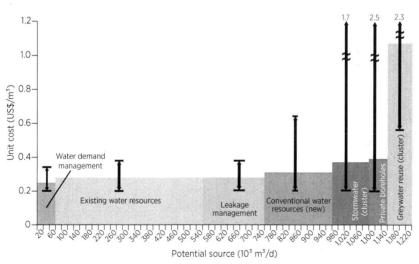

Source: World Bank.
Note: The range of unit costs (vertical lines) are based on the technologies and approaches used. For example, unit costs for water demand management depend on the quality and type of water saving devices; leakage management costs depend on the cost of water production and leakage control strategies; greywater costs depend on the treatment choices; stormwater costs depend on whether structural and/or nonstructural measures are applied; rainwater harvesting costs depend on whether simple storage tanks or pumping to elevated reservoirs are required. For cost assumptions and calculations, see Eckart et al., 2012. 10^3 m³/d = 1,000 cubic meters per day.

Some solutions are available at the household level. Public measures to support household water efficiency include requirements for water saving devices as part of building codes, provision of household water audits, awareness campaigns, and social marketing tools. These strategies are aimed mainly at high- and middle-income households. Building codes can enhance the effect in new estates. The whole potential from water demand management for households in Nairobi in the year 2035 is estimated at about 47,800 cubic meters.

One of the features of the IUWM approach is to identify areas or communities that can function as units for development (called clusters). Cluster-level solutions are particularly attractive in new development areas. A number of solutions—for example, in relation to stormwater management, greywater reuse, and leakage management—should be implemented at cluster scale to guarantee the reliability and high quality of the water supply. A cluster can encompass anywhere from a dozen households to estates/new suburbs with up to 50,000 inhabitants. The specific solutions available will depend on the size and sophistication of the cluster, but cluster-level solutions can be more cost effective than the same solutions applied at the household level. For example, in Nairobi, seasonal stormwater harvesting can be enhanced by providing a cluster-level reservoir that provides storage for three months of supply. Central storage for the whole cluster is more cost effective than if stored by individual households. For a cluster of 10,000 inhabitants with a density of 5,500 persons per square kilometer and a size of 182 hectares (0.182 square kilometers), a storage volume of 82,500 cubic meters must be provided. It is estimated that for the whole of Nairobi, a potential of 111,000 cubic meters per day in the year 2035 at a unit cost of US$0.37 per cubic meter is realistic (Eckart et al., 2012).[2] This might be combined with greywater recycling and leakage management at the cluster level.

Demonstration pilots can provide the best opportunity to test the opportunities and limits of a new approach. Upon request from Nairobi stakeholders, two locations have been discussed as potential sites for a demonstration pilot. One is Tatu City, planned as a high-income neighborhood; another is Konza Technology City, a 5,000-acre greenfield site at Konza and about 60 kilometers south of Nairobi at the main Nairobi-Mombasa route. In both cases it is proposed that initially the demonstration project should include just one cluster of about 100 to 1,000 inhabitants, and should include stormwater management and greywater reuse. This would test the applicability of IUWM approaches by manag-

Box 4.1

The Tatu Real Estate Project in Nairobi, Kenya: An Opportunity to Test the IUWM Approach

This megaproject involves construction of a new city of 62,000 residents, who will live in a well-planned environment of homes, office blocks, shopping malls, and industrial parks. Tatu is a privately financed plan. The US$2.3 billion real estate project could become a visible symbol of Nairobi's urban renewal and reaffirm Nairobi's position as East Africa's economic hub. The location—close to the United Nations offices in Nairobi and the leafy suburbs of Runda and Muthaiga—signals the intention of its creators to target the top level of Kenya's real estate buyers. A demonstration project in Tatu City would present a highly visible flagship and would have the potential for scaling up IUWM solutions. Initially, the demonstration project would include just one neighborhood of about 100 to 1,000 residents in Tatu City. The demonstration project would need to be developed in cooperation with the private developer.

Source: Eckart et al., 2012.

ing the water cycle as one system, matching water quality to its intended use, and potentially applying innovative technologies to harness the value of wastewater.

A demonstration pilot would be important to test the institutional capacity for implementing IUWM solutions. For example, reuse of wastewater and rainwater harvesting would both require changes in the building code for Nairobi. Reuse of wastewater might also require changes to the health code. A number of issues regarding who should bear the extra costs of measures, such as rainwater harvesting, if they were to be made mandatory for new developments, would also need to be considered. A demonstration pilot would require the collaboration of a number of agencies, institutions, and the private sector and would test the ability of authorities to collaborate in nonconventional ways.

Mbale, Uganda: A Time-Limited Window of Opportunity

Table 4.2   Key Characteristics and Location of Mbale, Uganda

Population (2011)	91,800
Estimated daytime population (2011)	200,000
Projected annual population growth	4%
Economic activity	Commerce, transportation, small-scale farming, and industry
Water consumption per person served (2011)	70 liters per capita per day
Utility water coverage	71%

Source: Eckart et al., 2012a.

Mid-size cities present an opportunity to apply innovative, well-researched, and well-constructed approaches to water management because they have little legacy infrastructure and are still relatively contained. But these cities are growing very rapidly and there is a limited window of opportunity to implement the necessary management structures. These cities also tend to have limited institutional and financial capacities, and approaches must be carefully planned to accommodate these limitations.

Mbale is located in a high precipitation area just west of a Rift Valley mountain range, where surface-water availability has traditionally been plentiful. But increasing human activities in upstream catchments have meant that the city now faces water scarcity issues during the dry season. According to Uganda's National Water and Sewerage Corporation (NWSC), the dry season abstraction amounts from the Nabijo and Nabiyonga Rivers together would traditionally be 2,000 cubic meters per day and from the Manafwa River up to 5,000 cubic meters per day (Eckart et al., 2012a). However, the intake from the Nabiyonga and Nabijo was discontinued in February 2012 due to lack of water. One of the major threats to the sustainability of the surface-water resources in Mbale is the unauthorized abstraction and pollution of water by the increasing number of settlements upstream along the Nabijo and Nabiyonga Rivers. NWSC officers note that a large number of people have recently moved and now live along the upper watershed of the Nabijo and Nabiyonga. The impact of these settlements is severe competition for river water with the NWSC.

Limited hydrologic information makes planning difficult. It was not possible to get river flow information for all the rivers that are considered as the main water sources in this study. Similarly, there was lack of information on groundwater potential in Mbale.

With an estimated tripling of the population from 2002 to 2035, water demand will exceed capacity of existing sources.[3] According to the census results of 2002, the total population of Mbale municipality was 70,437. The annual population growth rate was estimated at 4 percent, implying a population that will exceed 210,000 in 2035 or a tripling in a little more than 30 years.

Inadequate sanitation threatens groundwater sources. Many pit latrines are dysfunctional and overflow during the wet season, posing health risks. Stormwater drains are connected to the sewer and cause sedimentation and poor functionality of the wastewater stabilization ponds. Fecal waste management is a major problem in peri-urban areas as they lack even pit latrines and septic tanks. Although there are no data on groundwater quality, there are high risks of groundwater pollution due to infiltration from pit latrines. During the recent water scarcity event, people used local stream water as a coping strategy, and there was an outbreak of cholera.

The rapid spatial growth of Mbale provides great opportunities to implement IUWM solutions, but the window of opportunity is time-limited. The Mbale case study uses a structured approach to identify boundaries of future urban clusters (see Figure 4.5), identify additional water sources and prioritize their selection, select appropriate treatment technologies for promoting integrated water use, assess and balance water flows and contaminant fluxes within the IUWM strategy, and propose a cost-effective set of solutions. Separate and different solutions are proposed for legacy areas (mainly the existing core area of town) and new development areas.

Water security through diverse sources is a key solution. Mbale will have to rely on surface water, groundwater, and recycled water. Appropriate watershed management will be crucial to protect the surface water resources of the Nabijo, Nabiyonga, and Manafwa Rivers. This is a key aspect of the ongoing Uganda National Water Resources and Development project (World Bank, 2012c) and solutions must be implemented at the micro-watershed level. Groundwater will be protected by addressing the sanitation problem through a wide range of measures including public education, sanitation promotion at the household level, decentralized wastewater treatment systems (DEWATS), and soil aquifer treatment (SAT) implementation; these are appropriate sanitation tech-

Figure 4.5   Current Population and a Suggested Layout for Future Growth of Mbale Municipality, Uganda

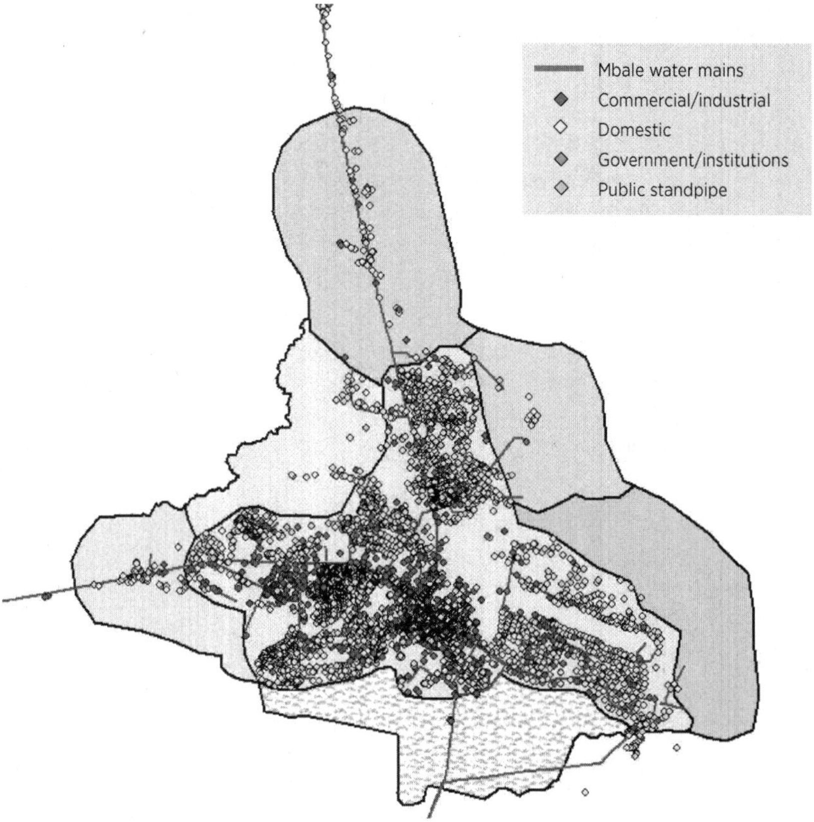

Source: World Bank.

nologies for a system that includes greywater recycling and groundwater protection. Note that public acceptance of these systems is addressed by discharging the effluent from the DEWATS into a SAT system, which then recharges the groundwater. Groundwater can then be extracted from the aquifer. In this manner a natural buffer becomes part of the recycling, making it more acceptable. There is only one potable water pipe entering houses, which reduces the risk of contamination due to crossed installations.

A possible combination of sources is illustrated in Figure 4.6. Note that surface water from the Nabijo and Nabiyonga Rivers is only calculated to supply 1,000 cubic meters per day, reflecting the increasingly seasonal nature of the flow in these rivers compared to the present. Surface water from the Namatala River, flowing on the outskirts of Mbale, has also been considered as a potential source (with up to 2,000 cubic meters per day capacity). However, even at this level, a strong watershed management program needs to be in place to secure the surface river sources.

Limited possibilities for retrofitting in the existing town center led the analysts to suggest isolating this as a cluster and apply only limited greywater recycling. It is suggested that the existing Mbale central business district be ring-fenced so that its central infrastructure system does not extend beyond its cluster boundary. By 2035 it is planned that 8,906 cubic meters per day for the central business district will come from the Manafwa River. The remaining water demand will be supplied by recycled greywater (951 cubic meters per day) from 30 percent of the high- and middle-income communities (which constitute 5 percent and 50 percent of the population, respectively). Hence, effectively, greywater recycling in

Figure 4.6   Staged Development of Water Resources, 2010 to 2035, for IUWM in Mbale, Uganda

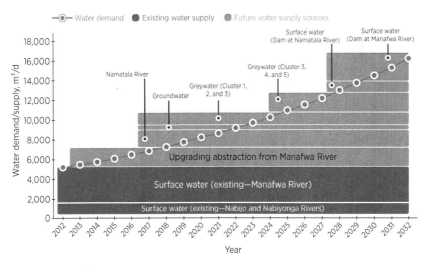

Source: World Bank.
Note: The figure shows the years at which the different water sources need to be developed to meet the growing water demand for Mbale. The volume of water supplies from each source has been determined based on meeting medium-term water demand projections. Some of the sources—for example the Namatala River, groundwater, and greywater for clusters 1, 2, and 3—might need to be developed at the same time. m^3/d = cubic meters per day.

this cluster will be practiced by about 16.5 percent of the cluster. Note that greywater never enters a household separately, it only leaves households separately and is then treated—see Figure 4.7 (Eckart et al., 2012a).

For new urban clusters a combination of surface-water sources, groundwater, and greywater recycling is proposed.[4] As these new clusters will develop almost from scratch, they provide opportunities to maximize water and energy-efficient water management options. The Mbale case study proposes for these clusters that water supply be a combination of

Figure 4.7   Schematic of the Proposed Water Supply and Sanitation System for Existing Built-up Area in Mbale, Uganda

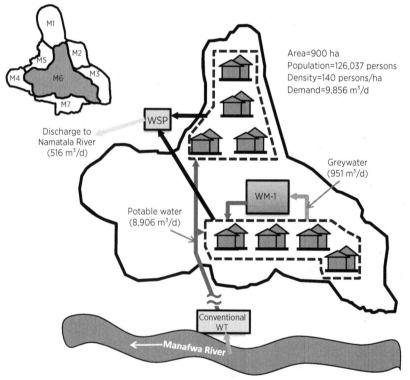

Source: World Bank.

Note: The figure presents the different technologies used as part of the proposed water supply and sanitation system for the existing built-up urban area of Mbale, Uganda. The top left-hand corner of the figure shows the existing built-up area M6 in dark gray. Technologies used in water management 1 (WM-1) were DEWATS with SAT and a conventional treatment unit (or with advanced treatment) for greywater recycling (for 16 percent of the population—high- and medium-income groups). Conventional water treatment (WT) unit was used at Manafwa River for surface-water treatment (existing). A waste stabilization pond (WSP) was used for wastewater treatment. Equivalent annual cost of proposed technologies is US$1,700,232. ha = hectares; m³/d = cubic meters per day.

surface-water sources (from the Nabijo, Nabiyonga, and Namatala Rivers), groundwater from a local well (at this stage only for cluster 5 due to lack of information), and greywater recycling for 75 percent of the population. Schematic presentation of the water supply and sanitation in Cluster 5 (as a typical example of the new clusters) is shown in Figure 4.8.[5]

The steps identified in the road map for implementation of the strategy were: acquire key information, create stakeholder platform, identify project champion, and design and develop demonstrations. The case studies carried out are only an initial step. It is important to recognize that

Figure 4.8   Schematic of the Proposed Water Supply and Sanitation System for a New Planned Development Cluster in Mbale, Uganda

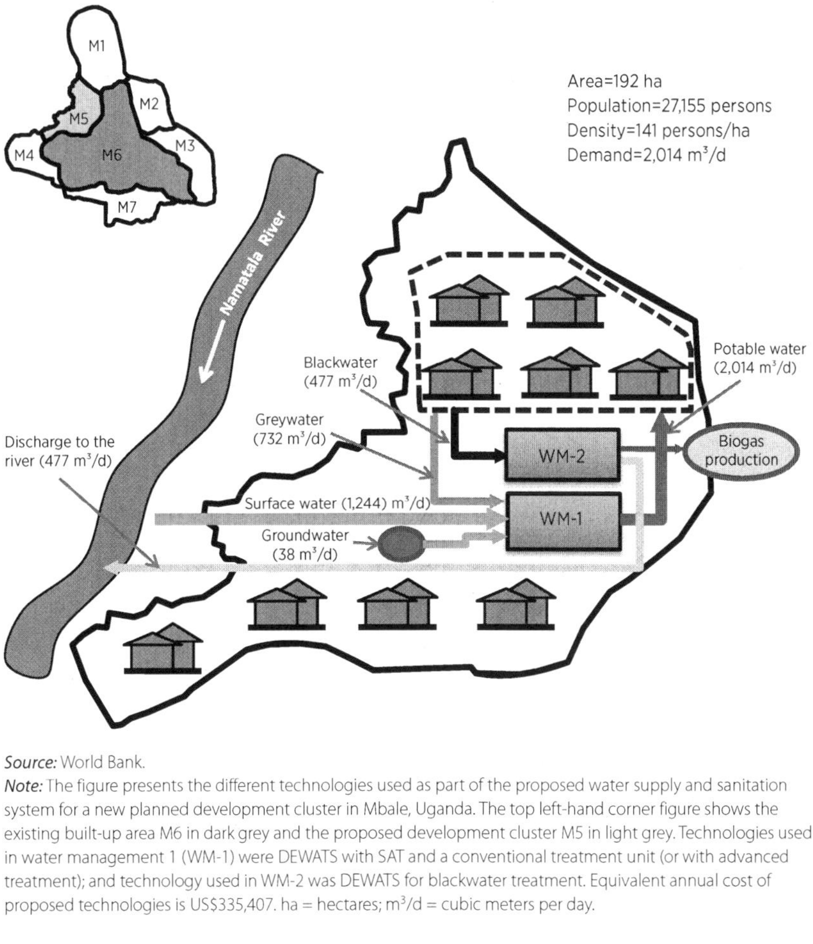

Source: World Bank.
Note: The figure presents the different technologies used as part of the proposed water supply and sanitation system for a new planned development cluster in Mbale, Uganda. The top left-hand corner figure shows the existing built-up area M6 in dark grey and the proposed development cluster M5 in light grey. Technologies used in water management 1 (WM-1) were DEWATS with SAT and a conventional treatment unit (or with advanced treatment); and technology used in WM-2 was DEWATS for blackwater treatment. Equivalent annual cost of proposed technologies is US$335,407. ha = hectares; m³/d = cubic meters per day.

urban form will impact the degree to which an IUWM strategy can be implemented successfully. Hence, it is critical that the strategy be considered early on during the urban planning phase of the emerging areas in Mbale and before the urban form is committed.

A project champion may already have been identified. Following the second workshop, the economic and sector work team received very positive feedback from the mayor of Mbale, as well as an email from the acting CEO of NWSC who requested identification of concrete next steps for follow-up.

Critical to the success of the roadmap (and the implementation of IUWM strategy) is the early and continuous integration of all stakeholders in the planning, decision, and implementation processes of the IUWM strategy. A formal Mbale stakeholder platform should be established early on, involving expert coordination, facilitation, and a process of monitoring and evaluation. This platform should be created with the support of the stakeholders already identified in this study (for example, city councilors, NWSC, urban planners, environment agencies, upstream community representatives), as it can build on the outcomes of the two workshops already undertaken. The stakeholder participatory process could adopt the learning alliance approach, developed during the Sustainable Water Management Improves Tomorrow's Cities Health (SWITCH) project (see Chapter 5).

Arua, Uganda: Can Decentralized Solutions Postpone a Very Large Infrastructure Project?

Table 4.3   Key Characteristics and Location of Arua, Uganda

Population (2011)	59,400	
Estimated daytime population (2011)	80,000	**Arua, Uganda**
Projected annual population growth	3.4%	
Economic activity	Farming, small-scale industry	
Water consumption per person served (2011)	50 liters per capita per day	
Utility water coverage	50%	

Source: Eckart et al., 2012b.

Unauthorized abstraction and pollution of water from the Enyua River by an increasing number of settlements upstream is a major threat to the sustainability of Arua's water supply. There are little data on these activities and information is anecdotal. According to information from local area NWSC staff, there are several settlements upstream of Arua town and many of these are located within 10 to 30 meters of the river bank. The majority of the settlements engage in subsistence farming of both food crops and animals, and large areas have been cleared of vegetation. Water is diverted by digging small open channels. In addition, there are small-scale industries (brick and tile production), which also divert water and generate sediment returns. As a result of this activity, as well as the construction of roads crossing the river, there has been extensive erosion with large sediment flows. NWSC reports that the diversion rate of water upstream of the city water works intake during the dry season can be as much as 70 percent of river discharge.

While there is a new regulation according to which no activity is allowed within 30 meters of river banks (NWSC, 2012), and while NWSC has attempted to restrict upstream water uses, it has been difficult to enforce. The authorities have recognized a need for a more participatory approach to watershed protection that includes diverse sources of water for the city to ensure water security and that considers the entire watershed in urban water planning.

The existing system is overextended in three ways: the water treatment plant is strained by the turbidity of the river; power supply is irregular, resulting in high costs and intermittent supply; and the network is overextended. The NWSC reports that the high sediment load damages pumps and reduces the efficiency of settling tanks and clarifiers. The town has a critical power shortage and the NWSC has been forced to use its own generator. This has resulted in high operational power costs of US$0.24 per cubic meter (NWSC, 2012). In addition, the power shortage results in interruption of operations due to lack of fuel for pumping. The intermittent pumping of water into the distribution network exacerbates cross-contamination of water supplies. The water supply network is currently being extended as far as Kuluva, which is about 11 kilometers from Arua. According to NWSC, the expansion is straining the capacity of the distribution system, and a number of locations are experiencing low-pressure conditions.

Improper drainage and wastewater management threatens drinking water quality. Current NWSC records indicate that the piped water supply covers about 50 percent of the residents. The rest use alternative sources such as boreholes, springs, and streams. According to the officials in the municipality, some of the residents dump their septic waste into pits overnight to avoid the cost of emptying by service providers. These practices are likely to cause groundwater pollution, particularly in areas where the groundwater table is high. According to a water quality survey by the consulting firm Cowater International (2005), all boreholes except two in Arua municipality showed heavy fecal contamination, indicating that aquifers are being polluted by poor sanitation. Furthermore, the town lacks a properly designed drainage system and during the field visit, a number of water supply pipes were observed to be crossing the drainage channels, thus being exposed to cross-contamination. Inadequate solid waste management exacerbates the challenge of contaminant ingress into the water supply system. This is because some water supply pipes cross the drainage channels that tend to be used as informal solid waste dumps, thus causing stale water to accumulate around the (less than watertight) water supply pipes. These negative interactions underline the need to view the water cycle as a single system in system planning, design, and implementation.

New surface water sources exist but are costly. One of the alternative surface water sources under consideration is 22 kilometers away from the town at Olewa, which is also the location for a proposed hydropower plant along the Enyau River (see Figure 4.9). Another alternative source under consideration is the Nile River, located about 40 kilometers from the town (Fred, 2011). Olewa can provide sufficient quantity to meet the 2035 Arua demand and the Nile can provide sufficient quantity for any imaginable demand from Arua. For this reason, many people prefer the

Figure 4.9   Map of Arua, Uganda, with Proposed Water Abstraction Points

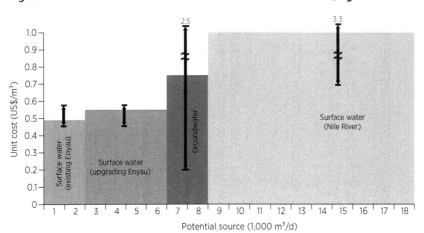

Source: World Bank.

Nile solution. However, the distance to the water—and more importantly the required lift—make both these solutions costly (see Figure 4.10). For Olewa the estimated lift required is 200 meters (according to Google Earth) and for the Nile River the lift is 700 meters.

Figure 4.10   Unit Cost and Potential of Surface Water around Arua, Uganda

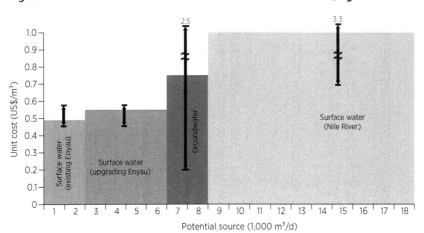

Source: World Bank.
Note: The ranges of unit costs (vertical lines) are based on the choice of technologies and approaches used. For cost assumptions and calculations, see Eckart et al., 2012b. m³ = cubic meters; m³/d = cubic meters per day.

Security and cost effectiveness can be enhanced through diversity and clustering. Arua has a diversity of sources that it can tap, and that might provide sufficient water. These include surface water secured through enhanced watershed protection, groundwater, water reuse through greywater recycling, and (to a limited extent) wastewater reuse. Based on unit costs obtained from NWSC, these solutions are all likely to be more cost effective than using water from the Olewa River (Eckart et al., 2012b). The cost and applicability of the solutions depend on local factors such as whether the city already exists or is expected to be built by 2035, socioeconomic status, groundwater well location, and topography. Eckart et al. (2012b) suggest an approach in which different clusters of Arua implement different solutions (see Figures 4.11 and 4.12). The cluster approach would be more cost effective because the system for each cluster would be designed to meet specific needs. More importantly, the cluster approach is adaptive and can respond to changing conditions in the future with more flexibility than a centralized system.

Protection of the existing surface-water resource is a priority. The viability of this integrated solution—and all other solutions except getting water from the Nile—depends on halting and reversing the negative impacts on surface water in the Enyau River from upstream activities. Upstream watershed protection and improvement are multidimensional

Figure 4.11   Unit Cost for Staged Development of Use of Sources for IUWM in Arua, Uganda

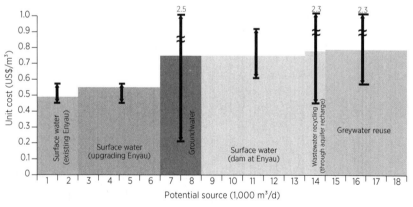

Source: World Bank.

Note: The ranges of unit costs (vertical lines) are based on the technologies and approaches used. For example, unit costs for greywater recycling and reuse depend on the treatment choices, and groundwater costs depend on borehole drilling costs and pumping costs to elevate the water. For cost assumptions and calculations, see Eckart et al., 2012b. m³ = cubic meters; m³/d = cubic meters per day.

Figure 4.12   Current Population and a Suggested Layout for Future Growth of Arua Municipality, Uganda

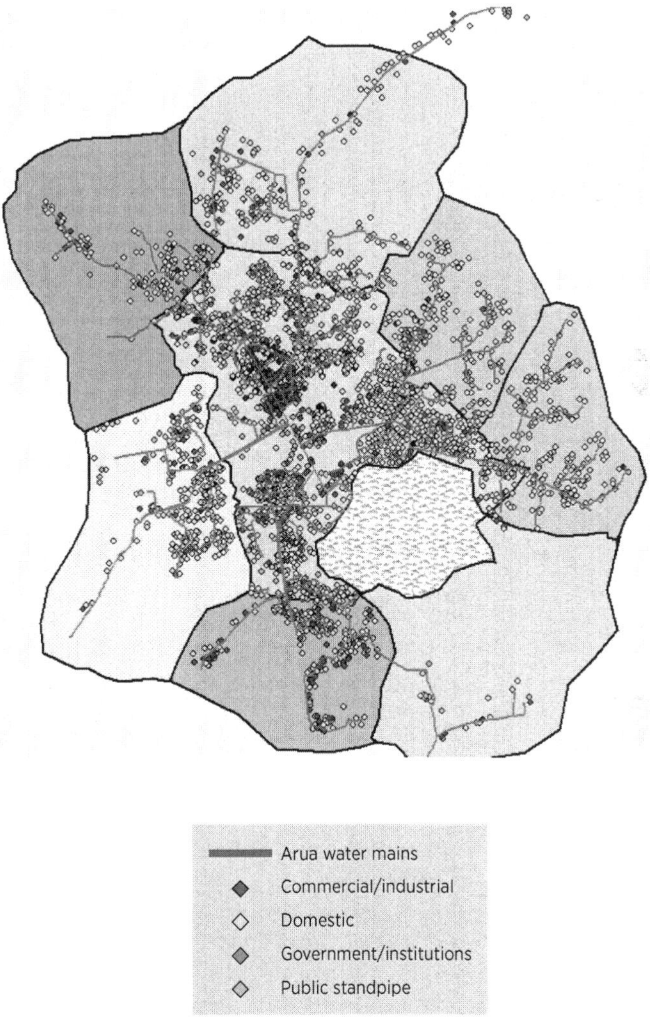

Arua water mains
◆ Commercial/industrial
◇ Domestic
◆ Government/institutions
◇ Public standpipe

Source: World Bank.

issues that require an integrated approach to socioeconomic, natural, and built systems. Watershed management and source protection activities are included as a key part of the Uganda Water Resources Management and Development Project. Active participation of all stakeholders will be crucial to success.

Groundwater has significant potential as a water source in Arua and its surrounding areas, but protection is key. Analysts (Gauff, 2011; Universal Water Consultants Ltd., 2011) have identified a large number of wells and suggest that yields are sufficient to augment the limited surface-water supplies. In accordance with the cluster approach to water management, Eckart et al. (2012b) suggest that where possible, each cluster have its own independent groundwater source. However, reliance on groundwater for water supply requires that the poor sanitation that is currently in danger of polluting groundwater be dealt with.

Water sources must be protected through integrated solutions. Eckart et al. (2012b) propose a system of greywater or wastewater recycling. In all cases households are only supplied with potable water and separation only takes place for water leaving households. In clusters, where there is surface water available for blending with recycled water, greywater is treated in DEWATS and then combined with treated surface water to provide potable water supply (see Figure 4.13 and Figure 4.14). In clusters, where there is limited surface water available for blending, wastewater is treated and used for groundwater recharge.

Figure 4.13   Staged Development of Water Resources, 2010 to 2035, for IUWM in Arua, Uganda

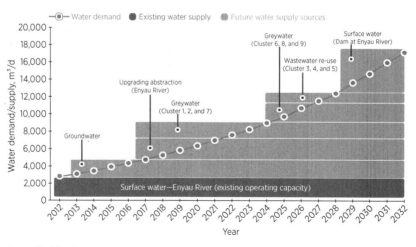

Source: World Bank.

Note: The figure shows the years at which the different water sources need to be developed to meet the growing water demand in Arua. The volume of water supplies from each source has been determined based on meeting medium-term water demand projections. Some of the sources might need to be developed at the same time (for example, upgrading abstraction from the Enyau River and greywater in clusters 1, 2, and 7). m^3/d = cubic meters per day.

Figure 4.14   Schematic of the Proposed Water Supply and Sanitation System for a New Planned Development Cluster in Arua, Uganda

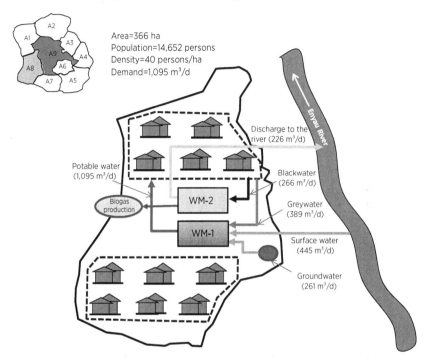

Source: World Bank.

Note: The figure presents the different technologies used as part of the proposed water supply and sanitation system for a new planned development cluster in Arua, Uganda, as a typical example of an urban cluster with access to surface water for dilution. The top left-hand corner figure shows the existing built-up area A9 in dark gray and the proposed development cluster A8 in light gray. Technologies used in water management 1 (WM-1) were DEWATS with SAT and a conventional treatment unit (or with advanced treatment); and technology used in WM-2 was DEWATS. Equivalent annual cost of proposed technologies is US$325,182. ha = hectares; m³/d = cubic meters per day.

The steps identified in the road map for implementation of the strategy were: acquire key information, create stakeholder platform, identify project champion, and design and develop demonstrations. It is crucial that the strategy be considered early on during the urban planning phase of the emerging areas in Arua. It is also critical that work on watershed protection for the relevant micro-watersheds be undertaken immediately before irremediable deterioration occurs.

Critical to the success of the roadmap is the early and continuous integration of all stakeholders in the planning, decision, and implementation process of the IUWM strategy. Similar to Mbale, in Arua, a stakeholder platform should be established early on, involving expert coordination, facilitation, and a monitoring and evaluation process. This platform should be created with the support of the stakeholders already identified in this study (for example, city councilors, NWSC, urban planners, environment agencies, and upstream community representatives), as it can build on the outcomes of the two workshops already undertaken. The stakeholder participatory process could adopt the learning alliance approach, developed during the SWITCH project.

Arua stakeholders have shown keen interest in concrete next steps. This might reflect the reality that Arua has an acute seasonal water scarcity and a water quality issue, and that conventional surface-water solutions will be costly. As was the case for Mbale, an email was received from the acting CEO of NWSC who requested identification of concrete next steps for follow-up.

Douala, Cameroon: Addressing Sanitation, Flooding, and Waste Management

Table 4.4   Key Characteristics and Location of Douala, Cameroon

Population (2005)	2,211,350
Estimated daytime population	—
Projected annual population growth	2.81%[a]
Economic activity	Industrial, commercial
Water consumption per person served (2009)	37 liters per capita per day[b]
Utility water coverage	40–60%

Douala, Cameroon

Sources: Biedler, 2012; a. UNDESA, 2012; b. IBNET, 2009.
Note: — = not available.

Current water management challenges in Douala are substantial.[6] Pressures on the city's water resources and services are on the rise as the city continues to grow at a rapid rate. This has resulted in a lack of safe drinking-water sources, increased pollution of water sources, local flooding caused by inadequate drainage, and associated health risks. In addition, institutional and governance challenges affect the way water is managed in Douala.

The poorest residents of Douala live in low-lying areas that are subject to flooding and contamination of shallow wells. These areas lie close to sea level and are near the coast. The areas are susceptible to increased runoff due to increased construction creating more impermeable areas, reduced rainwater infiltration at higher elevations, and improved drainage at higher elevations in the city. This has resulted in higher discharge peaks in the creeks and rivers draining to the sea and consequent flooding events—even with relatively low levels of precipitation. Flooding is further exacerbated by high tide events, which effectively reduce stormwater evacuation in the low-lying areas.

The main sources of water for Douala residents who are not connected to the city water supply network (which include the majority of the poorest inhabitants) are springs, shallow wells, and boreholes. Aside from structural damage, frequent flooding reduces water quality in shallow wells as contaminants are mobilized during flood events and are transported into water supplies. Sources of contaminants include overflowing latrines and solid, commercial, and industrial waste.

Poor access to improved sanitation in Douala creates large health risks for the population. The 2004 WHO burden of disease report indicated that diarrheal diseases caused by lack of sanitation and hygiene led to 18,300 deaths per year in Cameroon, and accounted for 13.4 percent of the burden of disease in the country (WHO, 2008). According to the 2010 data for the WHO/UNICEF Joint Monitoring Program, access to improved sanitation in urban areas in Cameroon was 58 percent (WHO/UNICEF, 2010). In Douala, cholera is endemic and coordinated action is needed to reduce and eliminate the incidence of cholera.

Wastewater and solid waste management services do not cover the whole city. The only sewerage in Douala is a six-kilometer stretch constructed before independence and that ceased operations long ago. The stormwater drainage network in Douala—that de facto serves as an open sewer—is not complete and not well maintained. The drains are regularly blocked, resulting in flooding during heavy rains and/or the regular presence of wastewater on streets and pedestrian pathways. Solid waste collection services are operational in some parts of the city (where the waste collection trucks are able to reach). However, a large proportion of the city residents (up to 50 percent) do not benefit from a waste collection service and hence solid waste is often dumped in the drains.

Lack of data on water resources in the Douala area hinder the management of the resource. A thorough analysis of the existing state of surface and groundwater resources in the watershed surrounding Douala has not been undertaken. It is therefore not possible to predict the impact of river-basin activities on the water budget or water quality for Douala. In consequence, it is difficult to carry out water resources planning and management activities for the city and to evaluate whether the existing water resources will be sufficient to meet the needs of the growing city.

A formal water policy paper does not yet exist, and the water law is outdated and not always applied. The foundations for water sector management are defined in the 1998 Water Law. This law recognizes that water is a national good to be managed and protected by the state. The law allows for the transfer of obligations for water management to local authorities and also allows for private sector participation for water services. Some principles of integrated water resources management are not mentioned in the 1998 Water Law. For example, the law does not allow for water management by river basin (or body of water). It does not make reference to integrated water and land management, nor to stakeholder participation in decision making. In addition, a formal water policy paper does not exist to guide the policy decisions with regard to water management. However, work has begun on a national integrated water resources management (IWRM) action plan.

A national approach to IWRM was initiated in 2005 when the government committed to developing a National IWRM Action Plan. Work began on the national approach under the Partnership for Africa's Water Development program with the assistance of Global Water Partnership and the Cameroon Water Partnership. A comprehensive analysis of the water sector was undertaken, and four baseline reports were published in 2009. However, the national IWRM process is currently on hold due to lack of funds.

The sector is characterized by top-down decision making due to a lack of intermediate government institutional structures, and there is a lack of horizontal input from water sector stakeholders such as the private sector, civil society organizations, and beneficiaries/consumers.

Decentralization of water management has begun, but issues remain. The government of Cameroon introduced decentralization in a 1996 amendment to its constitution. However it was not until mid-2004 that the secondary legislation was adopted by the National Assembly. Decentralization of water management started with the transfer of responsibilities for construction and management of boreholes and wells to the municipal authorities. Local governments are also responsible for drainage, although budgets often do not reach the local level. The state retains control of the urban water supply network systems. Presently, the state-owned asset-holder Camwater is responsible for infrastructure, with a private operator (Camerounaise des Eaux) responsible for urban water supply services under an affermage contract. The roles and responsibilities of the citywide municipality (communauté de Douala) and the district municipalities (mairies d'arrondissement) are not clearly defined.

There may be a need for an IUWM approach in Douala. As described previously, the city is experiencing rapid population growth, and there are many challenges in ensuring a safe water supply and increasing access to sanitation. The citywide municipal government (Communauté Urbaine de Douala) should take the lead in this, liaising with the central authorities and the municipalities at the arrondissement level. Some recommendations for a strategy to adopt an integrated approach are as follows:

- **Strengthen local capacity at the city/arrondissement level so that local authorities can participate more fully in project design and manage-**

ment. An analysis of the capacity (financial, human, technical, and material) of local authorities in the sector would be a first step in defining capacity-building activities.

- **Involve stakeholders in the water sector to achieve more sustainable water management.** Private sector, civil society organizations, and research/academic organizations do not currently have a voice in the sector. Recommendations to improve participation include undertaking consultations with stakeholders before important decisions are made with regard to design, implementation, and management of water activities. In addition, it is recommended that research carried out by local institutions be incorporated into decision making and planning.
- **Base decisions on the right data.** A lack of up-to-date and appropriate data on water resources and demographics make water planning and management difficult. There is a need to establish and maintain a comprehensive water information and knowledge database that is accessible to all relevant stakeholders in the water sector. It is recommended that the Ministry of Water and Energy, in coordination with Douala city authorities, actively promote the use of up-to-date information in decision-making processes.
- **Protect the quality of water supply sources through watershed management activities.** To help protect the quality of water sources in the city, a watershed management (river basin) approach is recommended—including providing a platform for information exchange between stakeholders.
- **Improve sanitation, drainage, solid waste management, and hygiene to reduce the risk of water-related diseases.** A combination of infrastructure investments in drainage and solid waste management, improved operation and management of this infrastructure, and promotion of sanitation and hygiene are recommended to reduce the risk of water-related diseases. This includes targeted hygiene promotion campaigns involving the water, health, and solid waste management sectors.

There has been no request for follow-up in Douala. This may be because the Douala study was a desk study with no face-to-face interaction with city decision makers; the ongoing contact that strengthened information transfer in the other case studies was absent here. It is probable that local interest in IUWM will require local-level understanding. Interaction with professionals and peers with knowledge and experience of IUWM approaches might well stimulate further discussion.

Participation of Stakeholders in IUWM: Experience from Case Studies

Three of the four case studies described in this book included a series of workshops and consultations with key stakeholders in urban water management (see Table 4.5). The initiative aimed at providing a forum for water sector stakeholders to assess alternative urban water management solutions and discuss the opportunities for implementing them in practice within each of the cities of the study.

During these sessions, it was confirmed that IUWM is perceived as a relevant issue by key stakeholders. Additionally, the workshops and consultation meetings also emphasized specific suggestions for concrete IUWM initiatives relevant for Nairobi and for mid-size towns such as Arua and Mbale.

World Bank experience in Latin America and the Caribbean indicates that at least 18 months is needed for stakeholders to coalesce around a strategy for IUWM. The expectation (again based on experience in Latin America and the Caribbean) is that three months after initiating the process, decision makers should be able to agree on a broad IUWM strategy for a specific city to be investigated further.

In Nairobi, the discussion revealed a strong interest from responsible authorities to enable the realization of alternative water resources for the city. This included positive interest in revising the building code to enable rainwater harvesting and to consider greywater and wastewater reuse, and interest in pursuing specific options such as rainwater harvesting and interest in implementation of a demonstration project in a new development.

In Mbale, the consultations focused on how a diverse mix of alternative and decentralized options can support improved wastewater and stormwater management while ensuring that water supplies are sufficient to meet future demand. Future approaches mentioned included the need to look beyond the city administrative boundaries and address developments within the local catchment. The need for greater institutional coordination and a strategy for enforcing planning regulations and guidance were also highlighted as priority areas for improving urban water management.

In Arua, a strong message was given with respect to the noninfrastructure opportunities that could play a large part in improving water management. Key among these is the application of watershed management to address the issue of increased water competition and unsustainable land use within the Enyau River catchment.

Table 4.5 **Stakeholders and Participants at the Workshops and Consultations for the Three Case Studies**

	Kenya		Uganda			
	Nairobi		Arua		Mbale	
Participant type	Water sector	Urban sector	Water sector	Urban sector	Water sector	Urban sector
Civil society and private organizations	Kenya Water for Health Organization	—	Association of Private Water Operators Uganda Water and Sanitation NGO Network	—	Association of Private Water Operators Uganda Water and Sanitation NGO Network	—
Subnational level	Nairobi City Water and Sewerage Company	Nairobi City Council	National Water and Sewerage Corporation, Arua	Arua Municipal Council Arua District Local Government	National Water and Sewerage Corporation, Mbale	Mbale Municipal Council Mbale District Local Government

(continued on next page)

Table 4.5 (continued)

| | Kenya | | Uganda | | | |
| | Nairobi | | Arua | | Mbale | |
Participant type	Water sector	Urban sector	Water sector	Urban sector	Water sector	Urban sector
National level	Ministry of Water and Irrigation Water Services Regulatory Board Water Resources Management Authority Water Service Trust Fund National Environment Management Authority Athi Water Services Board	Ministry of Nairobi Metropolitan Development Ministry of Planning Ministry of Local Government	Ministry of Water and Environment, Directorate of Water Development Ministry of Water and Environment, Directorate of Water Resources Management Upper Nile Water Management Zone	—	Ministry of Water and Environment, Directorate of Water Development Ministry of Water and Environment, Directorate of Water Resources Management Kioga Water Management Zone	—
International level	African Development Bank JICA (Japanese International Co-operation Agency)	—	SNV (Netherlands Development Organization)	—	—	—

Source: World Bank.
Note: — = not available.

Notes

1. For a detailed description of all scenarios see Eckart et al., 2012.

2. Assumptions of the study are as follows: Nairobi has two dry periods of three months each. Three-month water supply storage provides for the three dry months. The assumption is that stormwater collection would provide sufficient water throughout the year. For the detailed dimensioning of the storage reservoir, the real rainfall pattern would be used for the different locations of the clusters, as the rainfall in Nairobi varies significantly with location.

3. This will be caused by limits to infrastructure and resources. The capacity of the infrastructure needs upgrading in the near future (Eckart et al., 2012a). Even then the potential of the existing resources cannot meet future demand, especially during the dry season.

4. Greywater and blackwater recycling are sanitation options that also contribute to the water resources. In the peri-urban areas onsite sanitation systems such as ecosan and composting toilets have been proposed (see Eckart et al., 2012a).

5. Detailed information about population density, water consumption, and costs of implementation (represented in net annual costs) in the remaining clusters are provided in Eckart et al. (2012a), section 4.4.

6. Information for this section has been drawn from a desk study (Biedler, 2012).

CHAPTER 5

Making IUWM Work in African Cities

There is a growing sense among water professionals, municipal lead-ers, academics, and within the development community that a new approach to urban water management is needed (ICLEI, 2012; IWA, 2010; SWITCH, 2011; UNESCO-IHP, 2009; World Bank, 2010). In the words of an African academic: "Meeting urban water needs in the twenty-first century will require a paradigm shift. Nineteenth-century supply-side solutions alone will not balance the ever-growing demand for water driven by rapid urbanization, shortage of surface and ground water due to climate change, and competition from agriculture" (Awiti, 2012).

This book suggests that there are four ways in which new approaches to urban water management can be promoted, developed, and imple-mented in African cities: increase the use of integrated urban water man-agement (IUWM) in project planning and design, drawing on experience from other regions; generate more knowledge about institutional require-ments for IUWM; promote pilots to demonstrate IUWM in practice; and develop a learning alliance for IUWM in Africa.

Increase Use of IUWM in Project Planning and Design in Africa

Targeted grant financing to the initial planning stages of IUWM might be needed. In Africa, Azerbaijan, and Latin America, the World Bank's Water Partnership Program has funded the initial stages of IUWM planning for specific pilot cities. In view of the limited familiarity with IUWM, similar grant financing for initial stages is likely to be warranted until the concept becomes more generally known and accepted.

To make IUWM work in Africa, it will be necessary to address short-term needs, institutional constraints, and mid- to long-term development objectives. Strategies will need to be adaptable to the diverse conditions in African cities. Furthering IUWM in Africa will be challenging: it will require engaging and exploring new opportunities with city and utility managers; health, water, and other regulatory authorities; planning and engineering communities; and formal and informal service providers in both urban and peri-urban environments.

Successful implementation of integrated approaches with a long-term perspective will require early and active involvement of all stakeholders, including the end users, in particular in environments where enforcement of planning and regulation is often less than desired. Although stakeholder involvement might prolong project preparation, the involvement of a wide range of stakeholders could address political-economy barriers to integrated water management solutions. For example, in Tegucigalpa, Honduras, a coalition of commercial and household users and professionals have coalesced around an IUWM approach for the city that promotes good water management solutions and at the same time takes on vested interests. For each specific project, an early decision will have to be made about whether a longer (and possibly even less certain) planning period is acceptable.

The knowledge, attitudes, and practices survey conducted for this book illustrates that city leaders in Africa believe that integrated solutions (for example, for solid waste management, flood resilience, and water management) should be included in their future plans. Our case studies in Kenya and Uganda illustrate that city managers are interested in testing how spatial integration within cities and between cities and catchments can contribute to solving urban water management challenges. Investment institutions like the World Bank can proactively promote spatial integration within cities as well as between cities and catchments in its project dialogue with African clients. Some Latin American cities are already working with the World Bank to implement IUWM projects: São Paulo, Brazil, requested spatial integration of water and wastewater planning within the city to protect a key water source and reduce dependency on water transfers from other regions; Bogotá, Colombia, requested drainage, wastewater, and river bank rehabilitation to be integrated to address flooding and pollution issues.

Linking IUWM to investment projects is critical for success. Africa faces acute urban water management challenges. Unless IUWM is linked to investment projects, it is not likely to be perceived as relevant in Africa. Investment institutions like the World Bank can actively promote IUWM solutions in project funding and implementation.

Better Understand Institutional Requirements and Implications of IUWM

The principal challenge for Africa in the urban sphere is to address how its cities and towns respond to the massive challenges of rapid urbanization, urban expansion, increased demand for services, threats to water supply, constrained and failing urban planning systems, and institutional practices that work in isolation. This book argues that integration of decision making across sectors is critical for cities to cope with these pressures. The book also argues that sustainable management that prevents or reduces natural resource degradation, matches water quality to its purpose, recognizes that wastewater might be valuable, and increases resilience through adaptive systems, will be part of a long-term solution.

Unfortunately, we know little about the local-level institutional implications of the proposals to emphasize integration and sustainability. To gain a better understanding would require additional work at the local level. The questions in Tables 5.1 and 5.2 provide guidance with respect to the issues that should be investigated.

Table 5.1   Principles of Integrated Management: Evaluative Questions

Principles	Evaluative questions
Integration of resource sectors	• Is there a lead agency that coordinates land–water management activities, programs, or policies?
	• Are there guidelines or guiding principles for the achievement of integration?
	• Is coordinated implementation of management policies, programs, and goals achieved?
	• Is implementation of management policies, programs, and goals monitored?
	• Do implementing staff have adequate skills to implement integration?
	• Do implementing staff have adequate commitment to integration?

(continued on next page)

Table 5.1 (continued)

Principles	Evaluative questions
Integration of resource sectors	• Are there financial resources available that help to facilitate integration? • Are there support networks available that help to facilitate integration?
Coordination of government, nongovernment, and community management policies and activities	• Does a clear framework of coordination for implementation of management policies and activities exist? • Is coordination between government, nongovernment, and community stakeholders occurring? • Are stakeholders accountable for coordinated implementation of management policies and activities?
Stakeholder participation in resource management	• Are there opportunities for stakeholder participation? • Are stakeholders who should be involved in land–water management clearly identified? • Are the roles of stakeholders clearly defined? • Is equity maintained throughout the management process? • Do stakeholders have a strong role in the management process?
Accommodation and compromise	• Is there awareness about the potential problems of rapid development and the long-term availability of local water resources? • Are policies, goals, objectives, and means of managing development compatible with those of water management? • Are mechanisms in place to resolve conflict over the use of water in the event of drought?

Sources: Bloch, 2012; Carter et al., 2005.

Table 5.2   Principles of Sustainable Management: Evaluative Questions

Principles	Evaluative questions
Long-term objectives	• Has the long-term demand for and supply of water resources been assessed with consideration for the projected growth of the municipality? • Do long-term strategies for the balancing of development and water use within municipalities exist? • Is variability in water supply, due to climate change and changes in use of water, considered?
Wise and efficient use of water resources	• Are principles of wise use available?

(continued on next page)

Table 5.1 *(continued)*

Principles	Evaluative questions
Local solutions	• Is the amount and availability of local water supply known? • Do growth management strategies consider the availability of local water supplies? • Is consideration of water availability a condition within the development approval process?
Prevention or reduction of natural resource degradation	• Do management decisions take into account the long-term implications for aquatic habitats? • Do management strategies help to protect groundwater recharge/discharge areas?

Sources: Bloch, 2012; Carter et al., 2005.

IUWM could lead to a diversity of solutions that will create greater institutional complexity. The IUWM approach considers a diversity of solutions instead of assuming complete reliance on centralized water supply and discharge systems. Even when each of the solutions used might be technically simple—such as rainwater harvesting and sustainable urban drainage systems—dividing cities into clusters, each with a variety of possible solutions to be applied, will mean that more solutions must be considered by more authorities in more locations. After implementation, it is likely that maintenance of the systems will require different actions performed by more authorities in more locations than for a traditional centralized system. Careful consideration will be required to assess whether this added institutional complexity inhibits effective implementation of integrated solutions. It will also be necessary to determine how to build local institutional capacity to ensure that it is sufficient for effective implementation.

Implement Pilot Projects to Demonstrate IUWM in Practice

Demonstration projects are essential to raise awareness and gain a better understanding of how IUWM could work in practice in Africa. Implementation of IUWM is likely to raise a host of institutional, regulatory, political, and practical issues. Some of these can be foreseen—for example, the need to revise regulations to enable wastewater reuse and rainwater harvesting. But a number of unforeseen issues are also likely to arise. Demonstration projects will be an effective way to assess the potential benefits and drawbacks of IUWM solutions.

In three of the case study cities for this book, authorities expressed a keen interest in implementing specific demonstration projects. In Nairobi, Kenya, the focus of the authorities was on the selection of a new development estate to test aspects of water reuse and possibly rainwater harvesting. In Arua and Mbale, Uganda, the National Water and Sewerage Corporation (NWSC) suggested focusing on decentralized wastewater treatment systems (DEWATS), watershed protection, and the cluster approach to urban development.

Demonstration projects can serve as a bridge between existing water management projects and increased use of an IUWM approach in project planning and design. For example, in Guinea, Kenya, and Uganda, World Bank urban and water projects are near implementation stage. These existing projects could serve as a vehicle to move forward with the demonstration projects requested by city managers in Arua, Mbale and Nairobi. The IUWM pilots, in turn, would serve as a learning tool for the use of integrated approaches in future water projects in the country.

It will take time to implement IUWM approaches as on-the-ground measures. For example, the Latin America and Caribbean Region of the World Bank has worked on IUWM since 2009. An important part of their work has been to identify examples of good practice and to work with local authorities in selected cities to implement projects using IUWM. In Tegucigalpa, Honduras, significant progress has been made over an 18-month period in the development of an IUWM strategy (World Bank, 2011b), but analytical work is still ongoing and alternative measures are under discussion. Demonstration projects are a useful way to ease into the sometimes lengthy process of IUWM project development.

Promote a Learning Alliance for IUWM

Change will come mainly through local stakeholders, including city and municipal authorities, utilities, research institutions, and associations and networks involved in urban water management. However, change will also come through high-level bodies such as the African Minister's Council on Water. An IUWM network will support capacity development of personnel and institutions and mainstream the IUWM concept in the institutions that manage urban water in Africa.

An IUWM network would serve three purposes: the network would advocate the use of IUWM where appropriate, it would facilitate sharing knowledge and technology, and it would provide implementation support for providers of water management services. An IUWM network for

Africa would be a collaboration of various organizations including regional and local municipalities, educational and training institutions, nongovernmental and not-for-profit organizations, service providers (governmental and/or private), and utility operators. The network would also actively reach out to the communities that these organizations serve.

The operationalization of IUWM in Africa will need to be based on a range of models that address a diverse set of realities. The development and testing of these models will be facilitated by an IUWM Network–Learning Alliance. The alliance should include a diverse set of actors who can exchange ideas about what IUWM can mean for development and management of urban centers in Africa.

An IUWM Network–Learning Alliance for Africa can build on the experience gained in other parts of the world. The idea of learning alliances emerged in response to the widespread failure of new research to have a significant impact (SWITCH, 2011a). It was also a recognition that new products and processes are brought into use not just by the activities of researchers, but through the activities of a number of widely different actors and organizations. Many cities in Latin America have dealt with water management challenges in an urban transition similar to those in Africa. Much practical experience has been gained in relation to IUWM, for example in São Paulo.

South-South collaboration could play an important role in expanding knowledge about and use of IUWM. Networks of water professionals in Latin America are interested in becoming suppliers in South-South collaboration. For example, the Brazilian Water and Environmental Engineering Association is in the process of establishing a South-South Knowledge Exchange Water Hub with World Bank/World Bank Institute support. Comision Nacional del Agua, Mexico, and other organizations have also expressed interest in supplying relevant knowledge on water management.

The core target audience of an IUWM Network–Learning Alliance would be professionals involved in urban water and sanitation services, water resources management, and urban planning. However, because the measures that follow from an IUWM approach will need to be financed and publicly accepted, and might require changes to regulatory frameworks, it will be prudent to ensure close links to professionals from budgetary, health, and other relevant institutions.

For an IUWM approach to gain acceptance and be operational Africa-wide, higher-education institutions will need to change their curricula. In addition to curriculum changes, water professionals and urban planners will need to learn and update themselves throughout their careers. A learning alliance with a basis in a professional organization could be instrumental in providing training and education for professionals and in supporting higher education institutions in changing their curricula.

Several IUWM solutions, such as water efficiency measures and wastewater reuse, will need to be accepted by the general public to be effective. An IUWM Network–Learning Alliance could contribute information on water saving measures to primary schools and take other measures to garner popular support for IUWM solutions.

The World Bank could initiate the process of building an IUWM Network–Learning Alliance for Africa. Three options have been considered.

- **Option 1: Expand the scope of an existing network in Africa to include an IUWM focus.** The organizational memory and successes of an existing network could be harnessed to promote IUWM. A separate unit within an existing organization could be formed to focus on IUWM. Four existing networks that could host an IUWM Network–Learning Alliance have been considered:
  - **African Water Association (AfWA).** At present AfWA has limited capacity and no programmatic focus on IUWM. It can, however, play a supporting role in establishing linkages with leading utilities in Africa. Over time, an option could be for AfWA to develop a focused IUWM unit.
  - **United Cities and Local Governments of Africa (UCLGA).** At present UCLGA has limited capacity and no programmatic focus on IUWM. It can, however, play a supporting role in establishing linkages with leading municipalities and local government associations in Africa. It is collaborating with AfWA and a greater role could be foreseen in the future.
  - **International Water Association (IWA).** IWA is a promoter of IUWM through its cities of the future initiative. With a large membership of water professionals and a range of partners, it has adequate capacity to take on the task to lead a network. IWA has recently established an office with permanent professional staff in Nairobi, Kenya, and is well placed to create an active network of African professionals around IUWM.
  - **International Council for Local Environmental Initiatives (ICLEI)— Local Governments for Sustainability.** ICLEI is an association of more than 1,220 local government members who are committed to sustainable development. ICLEI already works closely with the World Bank on several urban initiatives and ICLEI Africa works with

the World Bank Institute on climate change adaptation. ICLEI has a number of members in the local government sector in Africa. While it does not seem that ICLEI has the capacity to undertake the leadership of such a network it would be an important supporting partner in the initiative.

- **Option 2: Consolidate a number of existing African networks in an IUWM initiative.** Existing networks in the area of water management and urban development can be brought together for an IUWM initiative. This could be done by getting selected networks to collaborate on becoming drivers of IUWM in Africa. This would constitute a loose IUWM-focused network that would be able to communicate across current institutional boundaries. The diversity of networking organizations could lend richness to the development and implementation of IUWM. There is a risk, however, that each organization would focus on its own priorities rather than prioritize the integration and sustainable management perspective inherent in IUWM.

- **Option 3: Create a new dedicated IUWM network by bringing together practitioners and experts with interest in IUWM currently working in a variety of institutions in different sectors.** A new organization would have the energy, fresh ideas, and momentum of a start up, given a skilled and enthusiastic support team. It would also have the opportunity to work across boundaries from the beginning. Transaction costs would be large, however, unless the initial support team is based in an organization with substantial existing capacity in Africa. A new structure will take time to get off the ground and might not be sustainable; sustainability would require long-term financial commitments as it is unlikely that membership fees would be able to finance the network in the foreseeable future.

Of these options, we recommend expanding the scope of an existing organization (option 1), as we feel that this will yield the fastest and most cost-effective results and be the most effective in promoting adoption at a local level. We suggest that IWA should coordinate the establishment of, and form the initial core of, such a network. However, there is a risk that a focus on a narrow set of interests (such as utilities and municipalities) would not take into account key stakeholders and issues (such as health and education). It is therefore recommended that a first step would be stakeholder mapping with the aim to ensure sufficient reach.

Funding will be needed to secure the viability of an IUWM Network–Learning Alliance for Africa. The Water Partnership Program has funded initial work with IUWM in three World Bank regions but additional financing will be necessary. Considering the emerging global interest in IUWM and the potential of IUWM to help solve key water challenges in Africa, it should be possible to secure financing based on a strong value proposition. Globally there are a limited number of centers of excellence for IUWM; some of those have been involved with this book. A future network should reach out to other centers of excellence, as well as to municipalities and utilities that have successfully implemented IUWM solutions.

Flowing Water in Fluid Cities: IUWM in Expanding African Cities

This book has argued that a new approach to urban water management is needed in Africa in light of the looming crisis of supplying water to a rapidly growing population. The complexity of challenges and the uncertainty about the future necessitate a more sustainable, more integrated, and more adaptive water management approach.

We have described what a more sustainable, more integrated, and more adaptive approach might mean in practice. This includes spatial integration, better coordination among institutions and across sectors, diversification of sources, and consideration of nontraditional sources of water such as wastewater reuse. In some cases this may entail decentralized and modular approaches. In arguing that IUWM could contribute to meeting the challenge, we have recognized that institutional and economic implications of IUWM are not yet well known. This is not surprising, considering that the concept is still relatively new, but more work is needed in these areas for IUWM to become the preferred approach in practice.

Appendixes

Knowledge, Attitudes, and Practices Survey—Methodology*

Objectives and Aims

Part of the assessment and diagnostic of integrated urban water management (IUWM) in Africa consisted of a knowledge, attitudes, and practices (KAP) survey on urban water management planning for decision makers and managers of African municipalities and water operators. The survey was inspired by previous work carried out by the World Bank Water and Sanitation Program for the Water Operators Partnership. In order to understand opportunities and constraints for IUWM in Africa, its principal aims were as follows:

- identify the perceptions of the current and future challenges of urban water management by cities and water operators in Africa
- provide information on the planning practices of these organizations.

The specific aims of the survey were to understand the following:

- aspects of current urban water management practices in Africa
- attitudes of cities and water operators to urban water management

---

* For more details, see Closas, Schemie, and Jacobsen. "Knowledge, Attitudes, and Practices Survey of Urban Water Management in Africa." World Bank, Washington, DC. Available at http://water.worldbank.org/AfricaIUWM.

- constraints to urban water management as perceived by cities and water operators
- similarities and differences of knowledge and attitudes between cities and water operators.

Survey Design and Dissemination

KAP surveys are designed to assess the knowledge that a selected community possesses on a certain topic. They also aim at revealing the attitudes and perceptions of that selected community toward the topic, and illustrate what occurs at the individual and organizational level as a consequence of such knowledge and attitudes (WHO, 2008).

A review of previously conducted qualitative and quantitative surveys conducted by the World Bank Water and Sanitation Program for the Water Operators Partnership on water utility services helped leverage some of the material needed to construct the survey. Additionally, a general examination of relevant literature on urban water management and the related documents helped design the survey. Previous work on IUWM such as the European Union's Sustainable Water Management Improves Tomorrow's Cities Health (SWITCH) project and publications by organizations like the Global Water Partnership (Rees, 2006) also helped define the issues relevant to assess opportunities and constraints for IUWM.

The target community identified for this survey consisted of chief planners and other senior managers of water operators and municipalities. A first version of the survey was tested as a pilot among five water utilities and two cities in January 2012. After the reception of the responses, the team modified some of the questions to clarify the scope and aims of some of them and to avoid double-barreled questions. Some questions had to be rewritten to include more specific instructions and wording. Some questions were deleted and new questions were added to help with comprehension of the questions and consistency in responses.

Survey Structure and Contents

The survey included a combination of multiple choice questions, rating scales with equal weights, and close- and open-ended questions. The questionnaire was divided into four sections. The first section was intended to identify the respondent: name of organization, title, and location. Section two was aimed at reflecting on the knowledge of the respondents to capture the main general aspects of the organization's current planning processes: if the city or water utility had an approved master plan, the planning horizon of the master plan, the stakeholders involved in the planning process, and the inclusion of 14 selected features in the current management plan.

Section three focused on the attitudes and opinions of the respondents regarding 23 specific planning aspects that could be included in the management plans of their organization. The aim of this section was to grasp the extent to which managers and decision makers in these organizations believed that certain features should be included in the management plans. It also sought to reveal the degree of belief by managers and decision makers in the value of a more integrated approach to urban water management in their planning practices.

Section four listed a series of open-ended questions with the purpose of extending the respondents' reflection on the topics and encouraging them to expand on the following aspects: what can be added to their organization's management plan, what problems their organization is currently facing with regard to urban water management, what are the constraints to achieve better urban water management, at what political or operational governance level the identified constraints can be resolved, and what kind of partnership can help solve the mentioned problems.

Dissemination and Response Rate

The team used the 16th African Water Association (AfWA) Congress in Marrakech in March 2012 to inform the participants about the Africa IUWM economic and sector work and the accompanying survey. The survey was designed and uploaded onto an Internet platform. The survey was also disseminated in paper form as an email attachment for use by respondents who had difficulties accessing the online format.

The survey was sent to 80 utilities in Central, Western, Eastern, and Southern Africa and 24 questionnaires were filled out, which represents a response rate of 30 percent. For municipalities, the survey was disseminated to 39 municipalities of which 13 finally responded, which represents a response rate of 33.3 percent.

Survey Responses and Representativeness

The selection of the sample for the survey was based on a combination of purposeful and convenience sampling methods. The inclusion of respondents to the sample was structured around their membership to two different organizations: AfWA and the United Cities and Local

Governments of Africa (UCLGA) organization. The sample selection also comprised some convenience aspects due to the fact that no proactive methods of data extraction were used. As a result, we do not know whether the sample is statistically representative of cities and utilities in Africa.

The decision to use these two organizations, to count on the active participation of their secretary generals, and to include the secretary generals as parties in this exercise was done to increase the survey response. The local knowledge possessed by these organizations facilitated better and more direct communication with the respondents and a higher level of exposure and dissemination of the survey.

The sample selected included a substantial representation of large cities in Africa (22 out of 34 cities having more than 1,000,000 inhabitants), but also a representation of small and medium cities (four cities having less than 100,000 inhabitants and eight others with between 100,000 and 1,000,000 inhabitants) (see Tables A1.1 and A1.2). The sample also reflected the different colonial administrative traditions of African countries by including an almost equal representation of Francophone and Anglophone countries (15 and 17 countries, respectively) and three Lusophone countries. Answers to the survey by water operators came from a combination of national- and local-level water utilities and an almost equal mixture of Francophone and Anglophone countries. Out of the 24 water operators who responded to the questionnaire, 9 were national-level water utilities and 15 were local. Among cities, Francophone countries dominated the responses received.

Table A1.1   Water Utilities That Responded to the KAP Survey

Country	City	Population	National/local level water utility	Language
Benin	Cotonou	882,000	National	Francophone
Burkina Faso	Ouagadougou	1,911,000	National	Francophone
Cameroon	Douala	2,348,000	National	Francophone
Côte d'Ivoire	Abidjan	4,151,000	National	Francophone
Ethiopia	Addis Ababa	2,919,000	Local	Anglophone
	Dire Dawa	256,800*	Local	Anglophone
Ghana	Accra	2,469,000	National	Anglophone
Guinea	Conakry	1,715,000	National	Francophone
Kenya	Nairobi	3,237,000	Local	Anglophone
Liberia	Monrovia	812,000	National	Anglophone
Mozambique	Maputo	1,132,000	Local	Lusophone
Nigeria	Abuja	2,010,000	Local	Anglophone
	Kano	3,271,000	Local	Anglophone
	Makurdi	297,398**	Local	Anglophone
	Kabusa	n.a.	Local	Anglophone
	Lagos	10,788,000	Local	Anglophone
Senegal	Dakar	2,926,000	Local	Francophone
South Africa	Johannesburg	3,763,000	Local	Anglophone
	Cape Town	3,492,000	Local	Anglophone
Tanzania	Dar es Salaam	3,415,000	Local	Anglophone
Togo	Lome	1,453,000	National	Francophone
Uganda	Kampala	1,594,000	National	Anglophone
Zambia	Lusaka	1,719,000	Local	Anglophone
	Ndola	455,194*	Local	Anglophone

Sources: UNDESA, 2012; *city population, http://www.citypopulation.de; **Nigeria National Census 2006.
Note: n.a. = not applicable.

Table A1.2   Municipalities That Responded to the KAP Survey

Country	City	Population	Language
Benin	Cotonou	882,000	Francophone
Cameroon	Yaoundé	2,320,000	Francophone
Cape Verde	Mosterios	3,598*	Lusophone
Central African Republic	Bangui	622,771*	Francophone
Congo	Brazzaville	1,557,000	Francophone
Côte d'Ivoire	Tiassale	19,894* (1988)	Francophone
	Treichville	170,000**	Francophone
Morocco	Rabat	1,807,000	Francophone
Niger	Diffa	48,005*	Francophone
	Tahoua	123,373*	Francophone
São Tomé and Principe	Sao Tome	49,957*	Lusophone
Senegal	Dakar	2,926,000	Francophone
Seychelles	Victoria	26,450*	Anglophone

Sources: UNDESA, 2012; *city population, http://www.citypopulation.de; **Reseau Ivoire 2007, http://www.rezoivoire.net/cotedivoire/ville/12/la-commune-de-treichville.html (accessed June 2012).

Copy of the Questionnaire Sent to Water Operators

1. General information

Q1.1	Professional title	
Q1.2	Name of organization	
Q1.3	City	
Q1.4	District	
Q1.5	Region	
Q1.6	Country	

2. Your organization's planning

In this section we ask you to answer the following questions about your organization's current urban water management plan.

Q2.1   Does your organization have an approved water master plan?

1 = Yes   2 = No   3 = I do not know

Q2.2   What is the planning horizon of your organization? (Please check the one that applies.)

1 year   2 years   5 years   10 years   20 years   Other (specify)

I don't know

Q2.3   Please specify which one of the following stakeholders are consulted before the approval of your urban water management plan (check all that apply).

- City's planning department
- City council
- Utilities regulator
- Consumers-users associations
- Other (specify)

Q2.4   Does your **current** urban water management plan include:

		Yes	No	Do not know
1	Drainage			
2	Bulk water supply (dams, storage, reservoirs)			
3	Water resources within your catchment			
4	Drought contingency plans			
5	Flood contingency plans			
6	Rainwater harvesting			
7	Consideration of competing users at the river catchment level			
8	Solid waste management			
9	Urban land zoning			
10	Spatial distribution of population			
11	Future population growth			
12	Informal settlements			
13	Roads			
14	The city's urban plans			

3. Your opinion on urban water management

Please indicate your level of agreement with the following statements.

Q3.1   The following should be included in the urban water management plan:

		Strongly agree	Moderately agree	Moderately disagree	Strongly disagree
1	Water network maintenance				
2	Sewerage network maintenance				
3	Water reuse				
4	Rainwater harvesting				
5	Water meters				
6	Solid waste management				
7	Wastewater treatment				

		Strongly agree	*Moderately agree*	*Moderately disagree*	*Strongly disagree*
8	Mechanisms for purchasing upstream water rights				
9	Permits for water abstraction				
10	Flood risk areas				
11	Drought contingency plans				
12	Water supply to informal settlements				
13	Sanitation to informal settlements				
14	Consultation mechanisms for water users and communities				
15	Conflict resolution mechanisms for water users and communities				
16	The city's urban plans				
17	Roads				
18	Future population growth				
19	Climate change				
20	Mechanisms to follow pollution standards				
21	Mechanisms to pay pollution taxes				
22	Measures to ensure environmental flows in rivers				
23	Monitoring procedures for drinking-water quality				

4. Open questions

Q4.1   List what else you think should be included in the urban water management plan.

Q4.2   Rank the three major problems your organization is facing with regard to urban water management (from the most to the least).

Q4.3   List the constraints to achieve better urban water management.

Q4.4   At what governance level do you think these problems can be best resolved? (Check all that apply.)

- Water operator
- Water resource management authority
- City council
- Regional government
- National government
- Other (specify)

Q4.5   List the type of partnerships your organization is ready to develop in order to speed up the resolution of the problems you have identified.

Copy of the Questionnaire Sent to Municipalities

1. General information

Q1.1	Professional title	
Q1.2	City	
Q1.3	District	
Q1.4	Region	
Q1.5	Country	

2. Your city's planning

In this section we ask you to answer the following questions about your city's current urban plan.

Q2.1   Does your city have an approved urban development strategy?

1 = Yes   2 = No   3 = I do not know

Q2.2   What is the planning horizon of your city's urban plan? (Please check the one that applies.)

1 year   2 years   5 years   10 years   20 years   Other (specify)

I do not know

Q2.3   Please specify which one of the following stakeholders or groups are consulted before the approval of your urban plan (check all that apply).

- City's planning department
- City council
- Private operator
- Public operator
- Utilities regulator
- Consumers-users associations
- Other (specify)

Q2.4   Does your **current** urban plan include:

		Yes	No	Do not know
1	Drainage			
2	Bulk water supply (dams, storage, reservoirs)			
3	Water resources within your catchment			
4	Drought contingency plans			
5	Flood contingency plans			
6	Rainwater harvesting			
7	Consideration of competing water users at the river catchment level			
8	Solid waste management			
9	Urban land zoning			
10	Spatial distribution of population			
11	Future population growth			
12	Informal settlements			
13	Roads			
14	The operator's urban water management plan			

3. Your opinion on urban planning

Please indicate your level of agreement with the following statements.

Q3.1   The following should be included in the city urban plan:

		Strongly agree	Moderately agree	Moderately disagree	Strongly disagree
1	Water network maintenance				
2	Sewerage network maintenance				
3	Water reuse				
4	Rainwater harvesting				
5	Water meters				
6	Solid waste management				
7	Wastewater treatment				
8	Mechanisms for purchasing upstream water rights				
9	Permits for water abstraction				
10	Flood risk areas				
11	Drought contingency plans				
12	Water supply to informal settlements				
13	Sanitation to informal settlements				
14	Consultation mechanisms for water users and communities				
15	Conflict resolution mechanisms for water users and communities				
16	The city's urban water management plan				
17	Future population growth				
18	Climate change				
19	Mechanisms to set pollution standards				
20	Mechanisms to set pollution taxes				

4. Open questions

Q4.1   List what else you think should be included in the city urban plan.

Q4.2   Rank the three major problems your city is facing with regard to urban water management (from the most to the least).

Q4.3   List the constraints to achieve better urban water management.

Q4.4   At what governance level do you think these problems can be best resolved? (Check all that apply.)

- Water operator
- Water resource management authority
- City council
- Regional government
- National government
- Other (specify)

Q4.5   List the type of partnerships your city is ready to develop in order to speed up the resolution of the problems you have identified.

Diagnostic of Water Management for 31 Cities in Africa*

Objective

City-level data for African cities are scarce. City leaders and decision makers within and outside cities need data to make informed planning and investment decisions. As part of the economic and sector work on integrated urban water management (IUWM), the World Bank undertook a major data collection exercise.

The objective of this diagnostic of water management for 31 cities is to contribute to better decision making by providing in one place an internally consistent overview of the current and future water management challenges facing selected African cities. The diagnostic also provides an indication of the institutional capacities that these cities have to deal with the challenges.

The diagnostic is presented in three forms:

- a city dashboard that provides an overview for each city
- a comparative table that illustrates the challenges faced by the selected African cities relevant to each other
- an IUWM capacities and challenges index.

---

* For more details, see Closas, Jacobsen and Naughton. "Africa Integrated Urban Water Management Index." World Bank, Washington, DC. Available at http://water.worldbank.org/AfricaIUWM.

This appendix documents the methodology, data collection, validation, and representation of the diagnostic. A full list of indicators and a sample of data sources are provided in Appendix 3.

City leaders and decision makers may also find Appendix 4, "Methodology for Urban Extent Maps," to be of interest and of relevance in making informed planning and investment decisions in relation to water. For the 31 cities, Appendix 4 shows historical and possible future spatial extent up to 2025.

Methodology of Data Collection, Validation, and Representation

The diagnostic was constructed through the following four steps:

1. Select cities to be included.
2. Select broad variables that are likely to have an impact on water management challenges.
3. Select indicators for each variable. In doing so, consider how the indicator represents the variable, data availability and quality, and process of data collection and validation.
4. Create tools for data representation.

Selection of Cities

The 31 cities (see Table A2.1) were selected based on whether they fulfilled some or all of the following criteria:

- population growth rate (more than 3 percent growth rate)[1]
- size (more than 2,000,000 inhabitants)[2]
- World Bank presence.

Table A2.1   Cities and Selection Criteria

No.	Country	City	Population ('000. inhabitants)	Population growth rate 1995–2010	Selection criteria*
1	Angola	Luanda	4,775	5.87	P,G
2	Benin	Cotonou	841	2.82	WB
3	Burkina Faso	Ouagadougou	1,324	7.02	WB
4	Cameroon	Douala	2,108	4.56	P,G,WB
5		Yaoundé	1,787	5.45	G,WB
6	Democratic Republic of Congo	Kinshasa	9,052	4.18	P,G,WB
7		Lubumbashi	1,544	4.06	G,WB
8		Mbuji-Mayi	1,489	4.47	G,WB
9	Republic of Congo	Brazzaville	1,505	4.19	G,WB
10	Côte d'Ivoire	Abidjan	4,175	3.29	P,G
11	Ethiopia	Addis Ababa	3,453	2.06	P,WB
12	Ghana	Accra	2,332	3.27	P,G,WB
13		Kumasi	1,826	5.04	G
14	Guinea	Conakry	1,645	3.30	G,WB
15	Kenya	Nairobi	3,363	4.08	P,G,WB
16	Malawi	Blantyre	733	n.a.	WB
17		Lilongwe	866	4.75	G,WB
18	Mozambique	Maputo	1,655	1.37	P,WB
19	Nigeria	Lagos	10,572	3.93	P,G,WB
20		Abuja	1,994	8.93	P,G
21		Ibadan	2,835	2.39	P
22		Kano	3,393	2.23	P
23	Senegal	Dakar	2,856	3.66	P,G
24	South Africa	Johannesburg	3,618	2.38	P
25		Cape Town	3,357	2.52	P
26		Durban	2,839	2.33	P
27	Sudan	Khartoum	5,185	2.53	P
28	Tanzania	Dar es Salaam	2,498	4.77	P,G,WB
29	Uganda	Kampala	1,597	3.72	G
30	Zambia	Lusaka	1,421	4.30	G,WB
31	Zimbabwe	Harare	1,663	1.30	WB

Source: World Bank.
Note: Selection criteria: P = population size (> 2 million); G = growth rate (>3 percent annual growth); WB = World Bank presence. n.a. = not available.

Selection of Variables

The selection of variables included in the 31 cities diagnostic is based on the existing knowledge and practices of IUWM. As defined in the book, IUWM adopts a holistic view of all components of the urban water cycle in the context of the wider watershed to develop efficient and flexible urban water systems. The variables chosen for the diagnostic focus on the aspects of IUWM highlighted in the book and present the main capacities and challenges for IUWM faced by major urban areas in Sub-Saharan Africa. For this exercise, seven different variables were identified that would best represent the challenges and capacities of IUWM faced by cities in Sub-Saharan Africa: urbanization challenges, solid waste management, water resources availability, water supply services, sanitation services, flood hazards in river basins, and economic and institutional strength.

Urbanization Challenges

One of the major impacts on urban water management is urban growth. Rapidly expanding cities will need sustainable solutions as they face an increase in water demand and expansion of water coverage. Increasingly dense urban areas will also need new planning tools to cope with the future demand of urban services and infrastructure. IUWM presents the opportunity to do things differently and to prepare for the future challenges faced by cities in Sub-Saharan Africa.

Solid Waste Management

By integrating urban planning with water supply and resource management, IUWM focuses on the linkages between different urban services and their impact on population and the urban waterscape. The lack of solid waste collection and management in urban areas can increase the risk of disease and health problems among the populations directly or indirectly exposed to the waste. Additionally, the lack of proper containment and management of solid waste causes environmental degradation as well as pollution of water resources through seepage and leakage from dumping sites. Poor solid waste collection can also increase urban runoff by blocking inadequately maintained drainage channels during storm events.

Water Resources Availability

The need to supply water to growing urban populations has to take into account the availability of water resources within the catchment in which the city is located. By considering the close link between water resources in the watershed and urban water demand, IUWM integrates these components across spatial scales. Urban population growth will put more pressure on existing water resources and will increase competition. In this case, exploring, diversifying, and planning new water supply sources under IUWM will reduce vulnerability and increase security in a scenario of climate change and potential future scarcity due to climate variability.

Water Supply Services

Water services and infrastructure capacity need to be planned in view of expanding demand due to population growth. IUWM incorporates traditional water supply technologies but also includes innovative approaches to help respond to the challenge of servicing more people. Diversity of water supply, new technologies such as wastewater reuse, and decentralized systems can help accommodate and adapt to growing demands and future challenges in urban areas. However, the current state of infrastructure must first be assessed to estimate future needs.

Sanitation Services

Lack of basic access to sanitation is a major cause of human disease and contamination of water sources. Dumping of untreated sewage, lack of collection, or poor wastewater treatment infrastructure can affect major surface and groundwater bodies for which cities are dependent on for their water supply. The challenges related to the lack of sanitation and the impact on water resources supply and human health can be dealt with by planning and articulating in a more integrated way the access to basic urban services by the population. The use in IUWM of innovative technologies for wastewater treatment can improve sanitation access and reduce the environmental and social costs of the lack of sanitation among urban populations.

Flood Hazards in River Basins

Urban populations living in coastal cities are exposed to storm surges and floods. Additionally, coastal cities also face a rise in sea level as well as the impacts of flash floods, storm damage, and coastal erosion. People living in flood-prone areas in cities will be more vulnerable to these challenges, and the infrastructure can suffer severe damages during these types of events. Due to the lack of storm drainage and the nondisposal of solid waste, flood events can increase the risks of sickness through the transmission of water-borne diseases in flooded areas and the contamination of water sources. Floods can also add stress to stormwater and sewerage systems as well as disrupt water supply and treatment systems. By integrating water resources, water supply, and city planning at both the city level and the watershed level, IUWM can help cities adapt to different intensities and frequencies of flood events by incorporating new technologies for flood control and stormwater management.

Economic and Institutional Strength

In addition to the previous six variables, IUWM also focuses on the potential of institutions to address the different challenges faced by urban areas. The potential of institutions to develop IUWM is linked to the management, and the institutional and legal capacities of cities and water utilities. For this reason, IUWM envisages close cooperation of water utilities with cities and key stakeholders to deliver services to larger sectors of the urban population. Adequate institutional and governance frameworks put in place by local and national governments as well as regulators and water utilities will ensure economic and socially sustainable urban water management.

Selection of Indicators

For the seven variables defined previously as relevant to future African cities in the context of IUWM, indicators were selected based on the following criteria:

- Indicators should be as representative as possible and cover all aspects of the variable (in terms of completeness, causality, and complementariness).
- City-level indicators were preferred so as to enable comparison between cities, and to present a more accurate description of the city-level situation. However, national proxies had to be used in some cases due to data constraints. Similarly, utility-level data varied depending on the utility's coverage; mostly, coverage was at city-level, but some utilities are national (for example, in Senegal). Nevertheless, for the indicators concerned (see Appendix 3), these proxies were assumed to be valid.
- Indicators that were available consistently for all or most of the 31 cities were preferred.
- Indicators were selected to be accessible and useful to the end user due to the target audience being both internal to the World Bank and external (city leaders);
- The indicator selection process was very much constrained by the availability, consistency, and reliability of the data for the 31 cities, which highlights the need to systematize such data for monitoring and planning purposes.

Urbanization Challenges

While population growth and urbanization are major drivers for change in Africa, indicators had to be at city level to make sense for this particular variable, which restricted the selection of indicators. The six indicators chosen (see Appendix 3) complement each other by illustrating both quantity and quality of urbanization challenges. The first four indicators quantify past, current, and future city growth in relation to national population growth, while indicators five and six quantify current city population in terms of pressure on urban infrastructure by looking at density and the share of population living in informal areas. Indicators for quantifying current and projected city population growth, as well as city density, came from relatively homogeneous sources (see Appendix 3). However, the last indicator (percentage of city population living in informal areas) came from a variety of sources and years, which leads to discrepancies in the data in terms of validation, definition, and consistency.

Solid Waste Management

It is solid waste collection and disposal, or more precisely the lack thereof, that impacts infrastructure efficiency by clogging drains, leads to health issues, and aggravates the effects of extreme weather events in a city. We looked for indicators that determined the lack of solid waste management both at household and business levels (primary collection) and municipal level (secondary collection). This corresponds to indicators seven and eight respectively (see Appendix 3). From this, the proportion of solid waste that does not enter the formal disposal chain can be derived and utilized for integrated urban planning. The lack of a single and comprehensive global source for solid waste management at city level for all 31 cities presented a problem, which restricted the number of indicators for this variable, and impeded efforts to quantify informal waste disposal more rigorously. Furthermore, the data used still presents some inconsistencies; for instance, data sources rarely indicated whether the percentage collected is on a wet or dry basis.

Water Resources Availability

As IUWM goes beyond the limits of the city and includes the water resources available for the city within a wider geographical context, water resources indicators were selected to encompass the following:

- Past and current water supply from precipitation (indicators 9 and 10) in the basin from which the city derives its water supply. These indicators are sourced from two databases, the Climatic Research Unit (CRU) of the University of East Anglia 3.0 database and WorldClim database (Hijmans et al., 2005).

- A range of indicators describing physical water availability in the basin (indicators 13, 14, 15, 16, and 17), which are sourced from the baseline data of Strzepek et al., 2011, and represent the period 1961 to 1999. As this baseline data is not historically observed but modeled data generated from the CRU 3.0 database, it comes with limitations (see Strzepek et al., 2011).
- The projected range of impact from climate change on specific hydrological indicators at basin level (indicator 11). This indicator is sourced from the Climate Change Knowledge Portal and combines the results of 23 Global Circulation Models for three emission scenarios. For specific limitations associated with the baseline data, the modeling process, and the resolution of the models, see Strzepek et al., 2011.

Water Supply Services
The current situation of water supply services determines how much more of a challenge it will be for the city and the utility to deal with an increase in demand for water at residential and business levels. This set of indicators was devoted to describing water supply services at city level in terms of the following:

- Capacity of current water infrastructure (indicators 18 and 19), which indicate how much of the lack of water access is due to poor infrastructure.
- Quality and quantity of water supply coverage (indicators 20, 21, and 22) for current population, which gives an indication of how future demand might increase in terms of consumption per capita as well as population growth.
- Financial sustainability of water utility (indicators 23, 24, 25, 26, and 27), which gives an estimate of how much more of a financial and management challenge it will be to expand coverage and supply for the utility.

Data from most of these indicators came from a variety of sources (see Appendix 3), which leads to inconsistencies in definition and consistency across all cities. The International Benchmarking Network for Water and Sanitation Utilities (IBNET) provided most of the data used to estimate the financial sustainability of utilities as well as water supply coverage and infrastructure. In cases where the water utility was national, it was assumed that it would service the main urban conglomerations and therefore was used as a reliable proxy to evaluate water utility governance at city level.

Sanitation Services

The lack of sanitation presents a challenge in that it impacts both human health, and water and environmental quality in growing cities. We therefore sought some reliable indicators to measure the lack of sanitation at household (primary) level as well as municipal (secondary) level in the cities surveyed. This corresponds to indicators 28 and 29 respectively.

The first limitation is that these indicators come from a variety of sources, which has implications on definition, reliability, and consistency across the cities surveyed. Secondly, it must be emphasized that access to improved sanitation does not in itself indicate that sewage is disposed of in a safe manner. As we had difficulties isolating an indicator for the disposal of all sewage, we decided to look at cholera prevalence as an indicator of poor sewage disposal (indicator 30). Again, sources are disparate and not consistent, and cholera is not only an indicator of extremely poor sewage disposal, but also of other factors including the resilience and efficiency of the health system, which we did not intend to capture here. Nevertheless, for the cities in consideration, it is the most representative indicator available.

Flood Hazards in River Basins

Indicator 31 selected for this variable was calculated for this study. It presents an estimate of flood frequency based on the United Nations Environment Programme (UNEP)/Global Resource Information Database-Europe (GRID) PREVIEW flood data set. The unit is the expected average number of events per 100 years (hydrological model of peak-flow magnitude). The methodology and sources used to create this indicator come from a variety of studies. City basin summary statistics are derived from the basin definition used by Strzepek et al., 2011. The frequency of flood events was created through a three-step process:

1. Use of GIS modeling using a statistical estimation of peak-flow magnitude and a hydrological model using HydroSHEDS data set and the Manning equation to estimate river stage for the calculated discharge value.
2. Observed flood events from 1999 to 2007, obtained from the Dartmouth Flood Observatory.
3. The frequency was set using the frequency from UNEP/GRID-Europe PREVIEW flood data set. In areas where no information was available, it was set to a 50-year returning period.

The data set was designed by UNEP/GRID-Europe for the Global Assessment Report on Risk Reduction. It was modeled using global data.

UNEP/GRID-Europe is credited for GIS processing, with key support from the USGS EROS Data Center, Dartmouth Flood Observatory 2008. The source for this data subset is the Dartmouth Flood Observatory, Dartmouth College. The data used to represent the level of flood frequency in the cities' river catchments is limited by the inputs of the hydrological model used. The data used the definition of hydrological catchments as defined by Strzepek et al., 2011, which presents limitations related to the use of satellite imagery in establishing land elevation and surface water runoff at the urban level that could include the presence of water infrastructure.

Economic and Institutional Strength

This variable includes institutional cooperation, transparency, efficiency, and the wider economic context needed to enable integration of urban services. Framing a useful set of indicators to illustrate this variable for the 31 cities proved difficult. Relevant information on institutions is fragmented and the realities of political decision making are also difficult to represent with indicators. Under this variable, we looked for city-level indicators that showed the levels of

- efficiency as indicated by the sophistication of current management of water and wastewater services (indicators 32, 33, and 34) and planning of current and future urban services (indicators 39, 40, 41, and 42)
- transparency of institutional oversight and scrutiny (indicators 36 and 38) for water resources management, and of country-level governance (indicator 44)
- cooperation between government institutions and water services providers (indicators 35 and 37)
- wider economic context (indicators 43 and 45).

Due to data availability, some specific indicators (38, 43, 44, and 45) are given at the national level as there were no equivalent data at the city level, but are assumed to be viable in the large cities under consideration. Sources were varied, ranging from World Bank data to the existence of formal planning documents for each city; therefore, specific planning documents might have been missed if they were not uploaded onto a public site. Some specific cluster indices were used (indicators 44 and 45), which also have their own advantages and limitations (see Appendix 3 for references). Furthermore, the Water Operators Partnership database is self-reported by the utilities, which makes it difficult to validate data.

Data Collection

The data used to create the indicators in this study was obtained through a process of exhaustive analysis of relevant published materials available on the Internet and produced by a wide array of organizations. Data collection was carried out in Washington, DC, between January and March 2012. The process of data collection followed two iterations. The first one included the initial review of the main sources of data identified by the research team as primary data sources. Once the initial sources were exhausted, the second iteration incorporated additional material from different secondary sources to complete the data gaps in the list of indicators.

Sources of Data

Due to the lack of a single or centralized source containing the data for the indicators, this study had to rely on multiple sources of information. Although data at the national level for urban water management are available (for example, WHO-UNICEF Joint Monitoring Program,

Table A2.2   Main Data Sources

World Bank sources	UN sources	Other international agencies	National public sources	Private and open sources
• PADs • AICD • IBNET • CSO AMCOW • Other World Bank publications	• UN-Habitat • UNDP • UNEP/GRID	• AfDB PADs • European Union • OECD	• International development agencies • Specific government branches (censuses, household surveys, ministries, and regulators) • Water operators (public)	• Dartmouth Flood Observatory, Dartmouth College • IWA Water Wiki • Wikipedia • Water operators (private) • Consultancies • NGOs • Research institutes • Academic journals

Source: World Bank.
Note: PADs, project appraisal documents; AICD, Africa infrastructure country diagnostic; CSO, country status overview; AMCOW, African Ministers' Council on Water; UNDP, United Nations Development Programme, AfDB, African Development Bank; OECD, Organisation for Economic Co-operation and Development; IWA, International Water Association.; NGOs, nongovernmental organizations.

African Ministers' Council on Water, country status overviews), the lack of city-specific data on urban water management made the task of creating the indicators and populating the sample of 31 cities more challenging (see Appendix 3 for a sample of sources).

Reliability and Quality of Data

The data contained in this general study of 31 cities has to be considered with a degree of caution due to general inconsistencies in definitions, measurements, and data collection methodologies. The inherent complexities of the sector, the difficulties in measuring institutional arrangements, and the validation of the data found added limitations to the data set.

The reliability of data and sources also affects the quality of the data used in this study and the different types of analyses that can be derived from the data. Following is a list of several of the main limitations affecting the data set:

- The different methodologies used by the different data sources add uncertainty to the data set.
- Different metrics and different definitions used by the sources add precision problems, which make the homogenization and integration of the indicators difficult.
- The use of different sources for the same indicator and different years adds inconsistencies and complications when homogenizing and normalizing the data to compare the different indicators.
- These limitations present a problem when trying to test the robustness of the data with different statistical methods or trying to use the data for more complex statistical analyses.
- In some instances, the data was self-reported, which limited its validity.

Validation of Data

One question that can arise from the discussion in this section is how can we be sure of the data's representativeness—in other words, does the data used in this study depict a consistent, useful, and rigorous story. This concern is even more pertinent in the context of Sub-Saharan Africa where the lack of data makes any new study a focus of serious and deep scrutiny.

The team is cognizant of the difficulties of finding good quality data for cities in Sub-Saharan Africa. The team also attempted to use global and regional sources where possible (for consistency) as opposed to specific documents and other reports where differences in definitions might constitute an issue for the data's consistency. In many cases, however, sources were scarce or presented methodological problems, and in some cases they were nonexistent. The team has maintained the highest level of rigor possible with the different sources used and in the data presentation and use in the study. However, due to these limitations different opinions about the choice of sources might still arise. The lack of data and their poor quality is also indicative of the necessity to explore and generate more data for Sub-Saharan Africa. Additionally, the need to generate more primary data on the state of water and sanitation at the city level is coupled with the need, as reflected in this study, to pay more attention to IUWM.

To overcome these problems, an exhaustive record of the original sources of data has been kept.[3] Descriptive and clarification notes containing the different definitions used and the sources have been added to the different outputs as well as to each one of the tables used. These notes try to be as detailed and comprehensive as possible although a degree of uncertainty still remains, due to the difficulty of tracking and annotating each one of the different metrics and definitions used. However, when the data presented some discrepancies, the information found was crossed-referenced and compared to other sources containing similar data to check whether the data found was within a reliable interval of significance.

Due to the variety of sources, discrepancies of data measurement can arise from this data set. During the collection of the data, when a problem of definition or measurement appeared, standardization was sought using generally and widely used definitions (for example, for improved drinking water we used data from the WHO-UNICEF Joint Monitoring Program). However, it has to be acknowledged that some differences and discrepancies might still remain within the data set due to the selection of the data sources.

Data Representation

Dashboard
The dashboard represents a subset of the data collected for the 31 cities in a format that would give the target audiences a snapshot of the current and future situation in the six areas identified for IUWM in Sub-Saharan African cities.

The dashboard has been constructed as follows:

i. Select indicators for the dashboard from the 31 cities database for each variable.

For each of the seven variables, indicators were selected so as to be as consistent and relevant for all the cities reviewed. The aim was to give a concise idea of the situation in each city as well as to show how each city fared in relation to some internationally established standard. Second, they were chosen so as to lend themselves easily to visual representation and enhance user friendliness. For instance, inter- and intra-annual precipitation data over a period of time were selected specifically for the dashboard.

ii. Add international benchmarks for comparison.

To give an estimate of the relative situation of water utilities in Sub-Saharan Africa, the dashboard also included a comparison of the individual city indicators with a fixed benchmark and the average of values for all 31 cities. The international benchmark for the operating ratio (operating costs to revenue ratio) for water utilities was set at 130 percent (based on Banerjee and Morella, 2011); for the collection ratio, it was set at 95 percent, as it was considered a realistic benchmark for bill collection (though a 100 percent collection ratio is considered ideal for best practice but rarely attainable). A benchmark of 25 percent of nonrevenue water was also considered acceptable. Finally, the benchmark for the future performance indicator was evaluated at 100 percent—meaning that the probability of the water utility facing financial difficulties in the next two years is nil, which is a strong indicator of best practice (Moffitt et al., 2012).

iii. Create visual tools to enhance end user accessibility.

To improve accessibility and comprehension of data, the dashboard incorporates a selection of visual tools to better represent the selected indicators and to monitor the information provided by the indicators at a glance. Graphic visualizations including different types of charts and graphs have been produced and customized with the purpose to better present to end users the data gathered. The objective of these visual tools is also to present different pieces of information together to identify the relevant challenges and capacities for each one of the cities in the study. By using colors, sizes, and shapes of figures, the dashboard also has the aim to increase the understanding of the information presented. The figures also show the trends and the progress for some selected indicators compared to the general average of the study sample.

Comparative Table

The illustration of the 31 cities diagnostic also includes a comparison of the relative position of a city in relation to the other 30 cities for a subset of the indicators, designed to reflect the areas that constitute current challenges and capacities. The comparative table enables each city to pinpoint its relative strengths and weaknesses compared to other African cities. The target audience is similar to that of the dashboard, but with added emphasis on local policy and management audiences. A subset of indicators from the original set of indicators used to study the 31 cities was selected (see Appendix 4); again, this subset was thought to represent six variables identified as central to IUWM, as well as reliable data that would be accessible to the target audience. The seventh variable on economic and institutional strength was excluded due to the fact that it included most of the national proxies used. Since this was a comparative exercise, city-level data was preferred and national-level data that had been used for the dashboard was deliberately omitted.

Methodology

A simple methodology based on the one used by the Economist Intelligence Unit[4] in their study of African cities was devised. This methodology was chosen for its simplicity and also due to the fact that it limited the level of normalization and aggregation of the indicators by allowing a comparison of the data indicator by indicator. The choice of this methodology also avoided ranking the cities or their comparison against an established benchmark, for it simply compares the values for each indicator for each city between themselves.

The data from the selected subset of indicators was then homogenized, and the mean and standard deviation for each of the indicators was calculated (see Table A2.3). The cities and their corresponding individual values for every subindicator have been assigned to one of five intervals depending on how much each of the individual values differed from the mean, plus or minus x times the standard deviation. Each city value has been normalized then aggregated into one single indicator, giving equal weight to each of the subindicators. The values were then classified on a scale of 0 to 4 and matched with the interval they belong to according to their aggregated values. The groups were classified based on different intervals calculated with the mean score and standard deviation as follows:

- 0 = below mean minus 1.5 times standard deviation
- 1 = between mean minus 1.5 times standard deviation and mean minus 0.5 times standard deviation
- 2 = between mean minus 0.5 times standard deviation and mean plus 0.5 times standard deviation
- 3 = between mean plus 0.5 times standard deviation and mean plus 1.5 times standard deviation
- 4 = above mean plus 1.5 times standard deviation.

Table A2.3   Calculation, Definition, and Codification of Intervals

Calculation of intervals	Below mean −1.5 × SD	Between mean − 0.5 × SD and mean − 1.5 × SD	Between mean − 0.5 × SD and mean + 0.5 × SD	Between mean + 0.5 × SD and mean + 1.5 × SD	Above mean + 1.5 × SD
Codification for normalization of intervals	0	1	2	3	4
Values for intervals	Between 0 and 0.99	Between 1 and 1.99	2	Between 2.01 and 2.99	Between 3 and 4
Definition of intervals	Well below average	Below average	Average	Above average	Well above average

Source: World Bank.
Note: SD = standard deviation.

IUWM Capacities and Challenges Index

There are many dimensions to consider when thinking of a city within the framework of IUWM: that of water supply as well as wastewater infrastructure, but also solid waste management, catchment condition, urbanization, governance structures, and so on. The variety of dimensions at the core of this approach make it difficult to compare cities to each other to estimate where the most pressing needs in terms of water-related management exist. The purpose of this index is therefore to describe the capacity and challenges of the 31 cities investigated in this report in relation to the multidimensional aspect of IUWM.

This index follows in the footsteps of approaches that have attempted to boil down multidimensional concepts into composite indicators, particularly in the sector of development, governance, and environment. A composite indicator is formed when individual indicators are compiled into a single index, which should ideally measure multidimensional concepts that cannot be captured by a single indicator (OECD, 2008). There is considerable literature on the merits and criticisms of composite indicators; for a review of the main composite indicators used to compare countries see Bandura (2008). Booysen (2002) gives an evaluation and critique of composite indicators in the field of development, which does point out that indices remain invaluable in terms of their ability to simplify complex measurement constructs. In the case of IUWM, the added value of such an approach is to get a holistic picture of the water-related challenges and capacities of the cities, which can then be easily broken down into its component parts, or water-related variables.

Methodology

In this index, cities were thought of as having two dimensions: water-related capacities and challenges. For each of these dimensions, the variables defined earlier as relevant to IUWM were categorized. However, not all of the indicators included in each variable could be thought of as belonging to the same dimension. For instance, the indicator for revenue water was thought of as illustrating the utility's capacity to deal with infrastructure maintenance and was therefore separated from other indicators for the water supply services variable, which remained in the challenges dimension. This explains why there are more variables in the index, though the indicators used all come from the same database (see Appendix 3 for the full list of indicators used).

Table A2.4   Variables and Indicators Representing the Challenges and Capacities of Cities

Challenges	Capacities
Urbanization challenges (1, 6)	Country policies and institutions (44)
Solid waste management (7, 8)	Economic strength (43)
Water supply services (20, 22)	Water-related institutions (35, 36, 37, 38, 39, 40, 41, 42)
Sanitation services (28, 29, 30)	Water utility governance (23, 25)
Flood hazards in river basin (31)	
Water resource availability (13)	

Source: World Bank.
Note: Indicators assigned for each variable in the index differ from the main database (see Appendix 3) and are represented here by the numbers in parentheses. For indicator numbers, see Appendix 3.

Data for both challenges and capacities were normalized from zero to maximum so as to facilitate aggregation. When needed, data was inverted prior to normalization, so that results were consistent with the overall message of the category (for example, percentage of the population with improved sanitation was converted to percentage of the population with no improved sanitation, then normalized, because a higher indicator value means a higher challenge for the city). When this was not possible (due to the unit of the indicator), data was normalized from zero to maximum first, then substracted from a total of 100 percent (for example, for water consumption, a high level of water consumption should be represented by a low value in our index as it represents a lower challenge).

Indicators were then aggregated as follows: each water-related indicator was assigned even weighting within each index dimension (challenges and capacity). The practice of even weighting for indices can be subject to debate but is corroborated by expert opinion (Chowdhury and Squire, 2006).

The limitations faced during the data collection process for the 31 cities general data set, and outlined in detail in the methodology for 31 cities database, also apply to the capacity/challenge matrix. Gaps in the data collected meant that for some cities, fewer indicators were available than for others, which affected the city's score.

This index is a preliminary attempt to illustrate relative challenges and capacities between cities and thus to inform decision makers of the greatest needs. It is hoped that the index will generate a dialogue to improve evaluation, and incorporate data inputs from cities and other stakeholders with the view to future improvements.

Notes

1. According to data from UNDESA, 2012.
2. UNDESA, 2012.
3. See database on http://water.worldbank.org/AfricaIUWM (forthcoming).
4. The Economist Intelligence Unit and Siemens, 2011.

Indicators for the 31 Cities Diagnostic*

---

* See 31 Cities Diagnostic Database, http://water.worldbank.org/AfricaIUWM.

Table A3.1 Selection of Indicators for the 31 Cities Diagnostic

Variable	Indicator	Type	Units	Dashboard	Comparative table	Index	Notes and sources
Urbanization challenges	1. City growth rate, 1995–2010	Quantitative	%	—	√	√	UNDESA, 2012.
	2. National population growth, 2010–2025	Quantitative	%	√	—	—	UNDESA, 2012.
	3. Share of city in national population, 2010	Quantitative	%	√	—	—	UNDESA, 2010.
	4. Share of city in national population, projection, 2025	Quantitative	%	√	—	—	UNDESA, 2010.
	5. City density	Quantitative	Population/km^2	√	—	—	Demographia, 2011.
	6. Percentage of city population living in informal areas	Quantitative	%	√	√	√	Various sources (e.g., UN-Habitat, 2008; UN-Habitat, 2007a; World Bank, 2010b).
Solid waste management	7. Percentage of solid waste produced collected (public and private collection)	Quantitative	%	√	√	√	Various sources (e.g., Parrot et al., 2009; UN-Habitat, 2010; UN-Habitat, 2011a; World Bank, 2009b).
	8. Percentage of solid waste disposed of in controlled sites (landfill)	Quantitative	%	√	√	√	Various sources (e.g., Parrot et al., 2009; UN-Habitat, 2010; UN-Habitat, 2011; World Bank, 2009b).

(continued on next page)

158

Table A3.1 (continued)

Variable	Indicator	Type	Units	Dashboard	Comparative table	Index	Notes and sources
Water resources availability	9. Intra-annual precipitation and temperature	Figure	mm and °C	√	—	—	Annual variation of mean monthly precipitation (in mm) and temperature. WorldClim climate layers (2.5 arc-minutes and 0.5 degrees resolution per pixel). For full methodology see Hijmans, et al., 2005.
	10. Inter-annual precipitation	Figure	mm/year	√	—	—	Deviation from mean annual precipitation, 1901–2006. CRU 3.0 database for 1901 to 2006 (approximately 50–60 km² per pixel). For full methodology see Mitchell, et al., 2003.
	11. Climate change impact	Figure	% relative change to base period	√	—	—	Statistics for a selection of parameters for three emission scenarios and 23 Global Circulation Models for the time period 2050–2059. Source: World Bank Data, Climate Change Knowledge Portal. For detailed methodology see Strzepek et al., 2011.
	12. River basin map	Map	—	√	—	—	World Bank Data, Climate Change Knowledge Portal. For detailed methodology see Strzepek et al., 2011.
	13. Average annual runoff	Quantitative	Million cubic meters (MCM)/year	—	√	√	World Bank Data, Climate Change Knowledge Portal. For detailed methodology see Strzepek, et al., 2011. Average modeled runoff at basin scale for years 1961–1999.

(continued on next page)

Table A3.1 *(continued)*

Variable	Indicator	Type	Units	Dashboard	Comparative table	Index	Notes and sources
Water resources availability	14. Basin yield	Quantitative	MCM/year	—	√	—	World Bank Data, Climate Change Knowledge Portal. For detailed methodology see Strzepek et al, 2011. Maximum sustainable reservoir releases within the basin for years 1961–1999.
	15. Annual high flow (q10)	Quantitative	MCM/year	—	√	—	Annual runoff exceeded 10 percent of the time for years 1961–1999. Source: World Bank Data, Climate Change Knowledge Portal. For detailed methodology see Strzepek et al., 2011.
	16. Annual low flow (q90)	Quantitative	MCM/year	—	√	—	Annual runoff exceeded 90 percent of the time for years 1961–1999. Source: World Bank Data, Climate Change Knowledge Portal. For detailed methodology see Strzepek et al., 2011.
	17. Groundwater baseflow	Quantitative	MCM/year	—	√	—	Sustained flow in a river resulting from groundwater. Source: World Bank Data, Climate Change Knowledge Portal. For detailed methodology see Strzepek et al., 2011.

(continued on next page)

Table A3.1 *(continued)*

Variable	Indicator	Type	Units	Dashboard	Comparative table	Index	Notes and sources
Water supply service	18. Total design capacity of water supply infrastructure	Quantitative	Cubic meters per day (m³/day)	√	—	—	Various sources (e.g., AfDB, 2010; IBNET, various years; World Bank, 2011c).
	19. Total production by water supply infrastructure	Quantitative	m³/day	√	—	—	Various sources (e.g., AfDB, 2010; IBNET, various years; World Bank, 2011c).
	20. Residential water consumption in city or utility coverage area	Quantitative	Liters per capita per day	√	√	√	Total residential water consumption, in liters per capita per day. Relates to population served by utility or population living in city, depending on the source. Various sources (AfDB, 2006; African Development Fund, 2007; IBNET, various years).
	21. City population served by utility	Quantitative	Persons	√	—	—	IBNET, various years.
	22. Percentage of city population with improved water coverage	Quantitative	%	√	√	√	Improved water coverage as per source's definition. Various sources (e.g., AfDB, 2009; IBNET, various years; World Bank, 2008a).
	23. Percentage of water sold by utility	Quantitative	%	—	—	√	Various sources (e.g., World Bank, 2008; IBNET, various years).
	24. Percentage of collection rate from population billed	Quantitative	%	√	√	—	Various sources (e.g., IBNET, various years; Pinsent Masons, 2012; World Bank, 2008).

(continued on next page)

161

Table A3.1 (*continued*)

Variable	Indicator	Type	Units	Dashboard	Comparative table	Index	Notes and sources
Water supply service	25. Percentage of nonrevenue water	Quantitative	%	√	√	√	Percentage of water produced and lost before reaching the customer, either through leaks, theft, or legal use for which no payment is made. Various sources: (e.g., IBNET, latest year; Pinsent Masons, 2012; Hove and Tirimboi, 2011).
	26. Utility operating ratio	Quantitative	%	√	—	—	Utility annual operating revenues/annual operating costs (IBNET, latest year available).
	27. Future performance	Quantitative	%	√	—	—	Inverse of the Water Utility Vulnerability Index (WUVI). For methodology details see Moffitt et al., 2012. The WUVI gives an estimation of the probability of a water utility to face financial difficulty in the next two years; hence the inverse estimates the probability of strong future financial performance. To create this indicator, the inverse is taken: i.e., a high value indicates strong financial utility performance. Source: IBNET, latest year available.
Sanitation service	28. Percentage of population with access to improved sanitation	Quantitative	%	√	√	√	Various sources (e.g., AfDB, 2004; República de Moçambique, 2011; World Bank, 2009a).
	29. Percentage of wastewater treated	Quantitative	%	√	√	√	Percentage of wastewater treated by treatment plant system of percentage of wastewater collected. Various sources (e.g., Mtethiwa, et al., 2008; UN-Habitat, 2011a; World Bank, 2011c).
	30. Number of cases of cholera from last outbreak	Quantitative	Persons	—	—	√	Various sources (e.g., WHO, 2011; WHO, 2006).

(continued on next page)

Table A3.1 (continued)

Variable	Indicator	Type	Units	Dashboard	Comparative table	Index	Notes and sources
Flood hazard in river basin	31. Frequency of flood events	Quantitative	Number of events/100 years	√	√	√	Estimate of flood frequency as the expected average number of events per 100 years (hydrologic model of peak-flow magnitude). Sources: UNEP/GRID-Europe PREVIEW flood data set; Strzepek et al, 2011; Dartmouth Flood Observatory, Dartmouth College.
Economic and institutional strength	32. Unbundling of bulk water production and distribution	Qualitative	Text	√	—	—	Two different entities responsible for bulk water production and distribution at national level. Source: Banerjee et al, 2008.
	33. Separation of business lines water-wastewater	Qualitative	Text	√	—	—	Separation of water and wastewater services from supply in urban area at national level. Source: Banerjee et al, 2008.
	34. Private de facto participation in water utility	Qualitative	Text	√	—	—	Participation of private utilities for water or wastewater service provision (participation in at least one of the two). Source: Banerjee et al, 2008.
	35. Existence of utility performance contract with government	Qualitative	Yes = 1 No = 0	—	—	√	World Bank, Water Operators Partnership database.
	36. Existence of regulator	Qualitative	Yes = 1 No = 0	—	—	√	At the national level. Source: Banerjee et al, 2008.
	37. Existence of water utility targets for access to services in informal settlements	Qualitative	Yes = 1 No = 0	—	—	√	World Bank, Water Operators Partnership database.
	38. Existence of river basin authority	Qualitative	Yes-No	√	—	√	Existence of river basin authority within the basin the city abstracts its water for supply (and year of creation). Various sources (e.g., Volta River Authority; Zambezi River Basin Authority).

(continued on next page)

163

Table A3.1 (continued)

Variable	Indicator	Type	Units	Dashboard	Comparative table	Index	Notes and sources
Economic and institutional strength	39. Existence of water master plan	Qualitative	Yes-No	√	—	√	Various sources (e.g., AfDB, 2004; República de Mozambique, 2011; World Bank, 2009a).
	40. Existence of solid waste management plan	Qualitative	Yes-No	√	—	√	Various sources (e.g., Lusaka City Council, 2003; République du Congo, 2010; UN-Habitat, 2010).
	41. Existence of urban master plan	Qualitative	Yes-No	√	—	√	Various sources (e.g., Cities Alliance, 2008; JICA, 2012; UN-Habitat, 2007a).
	42. Existence of wastewater master plan	Qualitative	Yes-No	√	—	√	Various sources (e.g., AfDB, 2005; Maoulidi, 2010; World Bank, 2007).
	43. GDP/capita	Quantitative	Current US$	√	—	√	Using national data. GDP/cap as a measure of wealth with lowest value = 0 and highest value = maximum for 31 cities. Values assigned range from 0 to 100%. Source: World Bank Data, http://data.worldbank.org/indicator/NY.GDP.PCAP.CD.
	44. Country Policy and Institutional Assessment (CPIA)	Number	Index unit	√	—	√	Using national data. CPIA is a World Bank cluster index measuring the quality of governance, national policy, and institutional frameworks. Values are from lowest = 1 to highest = 6, assigned values in dashboard normalized from 0 to 100%. Source: World Bank data, http://data.worldbank.org/indicator/IQ.CPA.PUBS.XQ.
	45. Human Development Index (HDI)/capita	Number	Index unit	√	—	—	Using national data. HDI is a measure of human development with lowest value = 0 and highest value = 1, assigned a value of 0 and 100% respectively. Source: UNDP data, http://hdr.undp.org/en/statistics/hdi/.

Methodology for Urban Extent Maps*

Objectives

City-level data for African cities are scarce and spatial information even more so. City leaders and city and other decision makers need data to make informed planning and investment decisions. As part of the economic and sector work on integrated urban water management (IUWM), the World Bank undertook a major data collection exercise. As part of this we developed (based on satellite imagery) a set of maps of urban extent for 31 cities in Africa. The maps show historic urban extent from 1990 (when available) to today and illustrate likely future urban extent by 2025. The purpose hereof is to contribute to better decision making by providing an illustrative tool of the likely spatial consequences of continued urban growth.

Methodology

Spatial modeling of urban growth has been developing since the 1960s, and has increasingly moved toward the use of cellular automata models. These models represent space as a grid where each cell in that grid is subject to a certain possibility of transition in use based on a defined set of spatial rules and probabilities. These simple systems can give rise to

---

* For more details, see Duncan, Blankespoor and Engstrom. "Urban Extent Map for 31 cities in Africa". World Bank, Washington, DC. Available at http://water.worldbank.org/AfricaIUWM.

complex dynamics across spatial scales and have been increasingly used since the 1990s following the increasing availability of computing power (Santé et al., 2010).

Four categories of urban models have emerged over the last several decades (Landis, 2001). In addition to cellular automata models, there are spatial interaction models that model choices for sitting firms and houses using economic and travel distance (for example, Wegener, 1998); agent-based modeling where a reduced set of representative decision makers populate the landscape and convert land uses based on a set of rules largely focused on the household- or firm-level (for example, UrbanSim designed by Waddell, 2002); and urban future models that model site-level transitions based on spatial relationships such as neighborhood statistics, distance to infrastructure, demography, economic conditions, and regulatory conditions (for example, California Urban Futures; Landis, 2001).

One particular model that has been widely studied and used is the SLEUTH model (Clarke et al., 1997). This model defines rules for cell transitions from nonurban to urban based on a core set of determinants and iterates over time. SLEUTH stands for slope, land use, exclusion, urban, transportation, and hillshade, describing the core input data sets that drive the model behavior. This form of cellular automata model simulates growth in time steps, and uses historical data sets to calibrate model parameters for forecasting in the future. Monte Carlo simulations are run and the results averaged to give a best estimate of future urbanization.

This modeling effort used a simplified cellular automota approach that was necessitated by limits in suitable consistent historical data over all cities, and a limit in computational resources. The first step in the modeling approach was to define the suitability of each cell to urbanization based on site characteristics and neighborhood relationships. Suitability was defined as a combination of enablers and constraints on future growth. The primary enablers of urban growth are proximity to existing urban areas and transportation infrastructure, while the primary constraints on urban growth are slope, water, and exclusionary land use zoning (Clarke et al., 1997). Population growth determined the area of suitable land that might be urbanized, as this growth is the primary driver of urbanization. Once the suitability rankings were mapped, additional populated areas based on measured urban densities and projected urban growth were allocated to successively decreasing suitability levels. Next, the stages of suitability calculation are described, followed by the method of urban area allocation.

Step-By-Step Description of Map Construction

Model Space
- Cells were defined as 28.5 meter by 28.5 meter squares, following work done by the Lincoln Land Institute (Angel et al., 2010).
- All data sets were projected into the Albers Equal Area Conic projection and aligned to a digital elevation model raster.
- All vector data were converted to raster data.
- The modeling extent was defined by a 20-kilometer buffer around the urban area from the most recent time period.
- All operations were executed in Python programming language or the ArcGIS 10 software suite using tools from ArcGIS 10 (Esri, 2011) and Python scripts.

Definition of Urban Extent over Time
- Primary input data sets: existing urban areas were defined through digitization of satellite imagery for 31 cities for three time periods (as close to 1990, 2000, and 2010 as possible for each city).
- Delineation steps:
  - The boundaries for each of the cities were visually identified for three different dates circa 1990, 2000, and 2010 from satellite imagery. The satellite imagery was Landsat Thematic Mapper or Landsat Enhanced Thematic Mapper (depending on the year) imagery data. These imagery data have a 30-meter spatial resolution with seven multispectral bands. The date and type of imagery varied between the cities. Table A4.1 at the end of this Appendix has the exact date and type of imagery that was used in the analysis. Also, each city boundary was projected in the local Universal Transverse Mercator (WGS 84, UTM) projection. The UTM projection for each city is also listed in Table A4.1.
  - Within the imagery, each built-up portion of the city (where buildings were visible) was identified and then a polygon was drawn around the visually identified area. The polygon was extended to areas that were within 1.5 kilometers of the neighboring area. Therefore, if a visually identified area of buildings had a gap between it and the next area went out over 1.5 kilometers, then these areas where not added to the city polygon. However if it was within 1.5 kilometers, then the area was included.

- The final outputs of this stage were vector polygons for each target time period (1990, 2000, 2010) showing the urban extent during that time period. See Table A4.1 for information about the imagery files used in classification.

Influence of Existing Urban Areas
- Primary input data sets: urban extent delineations from previous step.
- Modeling steps:
  - Concentric zones were defined around the most recent urban extent at distances of 5, 10, 25, and 60 cells (some cities used 40 cells as the outer extent).
  - Cells in each zone were weighted less the further away from the existing urban areas they fell. These weights were 100 for the closest ring, 75 for the next closest ring, 50 for the next closest, and 25 for the outer ring.
- The final output of this step is the urban influence raster.

Influence of Roads
- Primary input data sets: Open Street Map data from 2011 (Open Street Map, 2011). All roads were considered regardless of type, except for Capetown, Durban, and Johannesburg, where road data comes from the Africa Infrastructure Country Diagnostic (AICD N.D.).
- Modeling steps:
  - The influence of roads was determined by the location of existing roads, the cells immediately adjacent to existing roads, and cells within a certain buffer distance of existing roads.
  - Road cells themselves were defined as unsuitable for urbanization.
  - A buffer distance of 15 cells was used to define near-road areas.
- The final outputs of this stage were three rasters—roads, next-to-roads, and near-roads.

Influence of Slope
- Primary input data sets: 90-meter void-filled Shuttle Radar Topographic Mission (SRTM) digital elevation model developed by the Consultative Group on International Agricultural Research (CGIAR) (Jarvis et al., 2008), except for Accra, where HydroSHEDS 90-meter void-filled SRTM data (Lehner et al., 2008) were used.
- Modeling steps:
  - Slope was calculated from the elevation data and resampled to model resolution.

- – Cells with slopes greater than a 100 percent rise were considered impossible to urbanize (that is, they were given a weight of 0).
- – Cells between 25 percent and 100 percent were considered difficult to urbanize, and were given a weight of 50.
- – Cells between 0 and 25 percent were considered easy to urbanize, and given a weight of 100.
- The final output of this stage was a raster classifying pixels into one of three categories of slope.

Influence of Exclusions
- Exclusions were defined as national parks, water bodies, and existing urban areas.
- Primary input data sets:
  - – Water: Modis IGBP (International Geosphere-Biosphere Programme) landcover data (Schneider et al., 2009) and the Global Reservoirs and Dams database (Lehner et al., 2011);
  - – National parks: World Protected Areas Database (IUCN and UNEP, 2010), specifically all reserves with IUCN category status of Ia, Ib, or II;
- Modeling steps:
  - – Resample landcover data set to model resolution.
  - – Convert landcover to binary water/not-water classification.
  - – Convert reservoir data to binary water/not-water classification.
  - – Combine these with urban/not urban classification.
- The result of this stage is a raster of cells showing where development will be excluded, which was binary and thus not weighted.

Calculating Suitability
- The derived data sets from the previous sets (urban, slope, road, next-to-road, near-road, and exclusions) were combined with relative weights to create a suitability score for each pixel.
- The equation used was:
  - – Suitability = Exclude × (SlopeWeight × Slope + UrbanWeight × Urban + (RoadNextWeight × Next-To-Road + RoadNearWeight × Near-Road)).
  - – The following user-defined parameters were used for all runs:
    - o SlopeWeight = 50
    - o UrbanWeight = 100
    - o RoadNextWeight = 75
    - o RoadNearWeight = 40.

Allocating a New Urban Area
- The final stage calculated a potential new area needed to accommodate anticipated population growth at a defined density.
- Input data sets:
  - Urban density: Demographia measurements of urban densities in 2011 (Demographia, 2011) for all 31 cities. Lacking consistent data, these density levels were assumed to remain unchanged into 2025.
  - Population growth: UN population estimates (UNDESA, 2011) for all cities but Blantyre were obtained for 2010 and 2025. Blantyre was too small, so Demographia data on Blantyre's 2010 population was combined with Lilongwe's annual growth rate to generate approximate population pressure into 2025.
- Modeling steps:
  - Calculate expected population change.
  - Use density to calculate new urban area needed in number of cells.
  - Starting with highest suitability, assign all cells as urban in each decreasing suitability level until reaching the suitability level where there are more cells available than required to meet demand.
  - For this final suitability level, allocate remaining needed pixels randomly.

Post-Modeling Adjustments to Displayed Urban Growth Potential
- Cut out rivers.
- Erase obvious places where effect of barrier was not captured.
- In cases where area was allocated to large areas of low suitability, creating very dispersed random placements of pixels, this last stage of allocation was removed from the final display (see room for improvement).

Post-Modeling Adjustments to Displayed Urban Growth Potential
In general, the results of this modeling exercise should not be taken as assertions about where development *will* happen, but rather those areas *most likely* to be urbanized by 2025. The goal was to use some basic spatial characteristics of the context of each city to develop a more nuanced picture of where growth may happen than could be achieved just by assuming uniform expansion. Some specific limitations include:

- Roads
  - We did not model changes in transportation infrastructure.

- We did not model roads as rigorous spatial networks, so travel times along roads could not be considered, only straight-line distances to existing urban areas.
- We did not consider differences in road quality.
- Urban area
  - The choice of what constitutes "urban" involves some subjectivity when doing digitization from imagery, as well as choosing which satellite settlements to include as part of the named urban area.
- Barriers
  - Barriers to the movement of people, such as a large river, were not incorporated in the model, as the primary consideration was proximity, not how a cell would be accessed.
- Water
  - The landcover data used is very coarse, and may miss smaller water bodies that are nonetheless important for constraining urbanization.
- Zoning
  - Land use conversions are highly dependent on regulatory regimes such as land use zoning, which could not be captured here because of inadequate, comparable data.
- Other exclusions
  - Due to a lack of consistent and readily available data, we did not include swamps or airports in these simulations.

Room for Improvement

As this modeling effort was a quick pass to illustrate the potential impact that future urbanization could have on nearby water resources, there are a number of ways that the approach and results could be improved. Particular options include:

- Sensitivity analysis and more rigorous parameterization would improve the model.
- As a last step of urbanization allocation, the lowest suitability zone to be urbanized has pixels assigned randomly, with no consideration of spatial neighborhood—it would be better to preference cells closer to the city for random allocation (that is, density decay grid).
- Road quality, such as the difference between roads connecting secondary cities versus minor roads, may provide additional spatial information on the suitability of urban growth along these different types of roads.

- The change of density can be calculated from the UN population data for the urban extent year of record. A density measure of the historical data could provide additional insight and better parameterization of the model for projecting future changes.

Additional Cartographic References

In addition, each map made cartographic use of the following data sets:

Dams and reservoirs:
Lehner, B., C. Reidy Liermann, C. Revenga, C. Vörösmarty, B. Fekete, P. Crouzet, P. Döll, M. Endejan, K. Frenken, J. Magome C. Nilsson, J. Robertson, R. Rödel, N. Sindorf, and D. Wisser. 2011. "High Resolution Mapping of the World's Reservoirs and Dams for Sustainable River Flow Management." *Frontiers in Ecology and the Environment* 9(9): 494–502. Available online at http://www.gwsp.org/85.html.

Rivers:
For South African cities: *Rivers of South Africa at 1:500000 Scale.* Resource Quality Services and Chief Directorate of National Geo-Spatial Information, Department of Water Affairs, Republic of South Africa. Last updated in 2003. Available online at http://www.dwaf.gov.za/iwqs/gis_data/river/All.html.

For all other cities: USGS HydroSHEDS, described in Lehner, B., K. Verdin, and A. Jarvis. 2008. "New Global Hydrography Derived from Spaceborne Elevation Data." *Eos, Transactions, AGU* 89(10): 93–94. Available online at http://www.worldwildlife.org/hydrosheds.

Major towns:
Location and population data set created by MaxMind, available from http://www.maxmind.com/; using population data compiled by *World Gazetteer*, and available online at http://world-gazetteer.com/.

Political boundaries:
National boundaries come from Esri's World Countries data set. Last updated November 2011. Available online at http://www.arcgis.com/home/item.html?id=3864c63872d84aec91933618e3815dd2.

Illustrating the Modeling Process, using Kumasi, Ghana, as an Example*

Figure A4.1   Initial Landscape

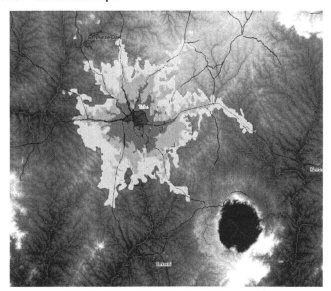

Figure A4.2   Influence of Roads: Next-to-Road

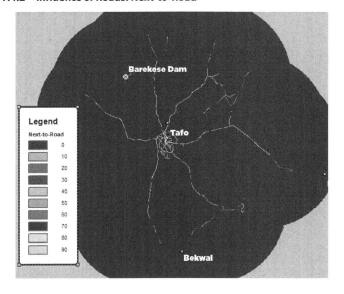

---

* For the urban extent maps of all 31 cities, see http://water.worldbank.org/AfricaIUWM.

Figure A4.3   Influence of Roads: Near Road

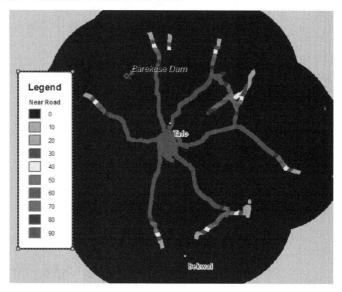

Figure A4.4   Influence of Slope: Slope Ranking

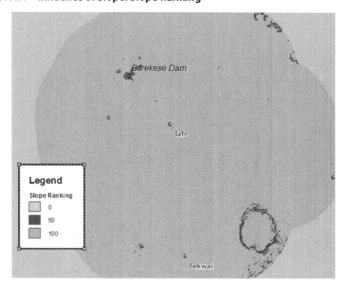

Figure A4.5   Excluded Areas: Exclusion Binary Ranking

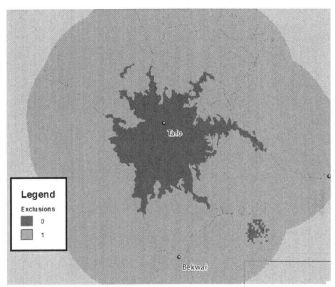

Figure A4.6   Suitability Ranking for Urbanization

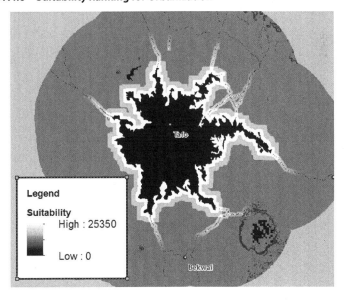

Figure A4.7   New Area Allocated to Urban Use

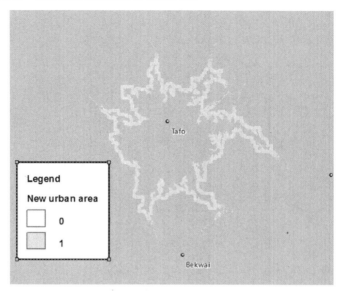

Figure A4.8   Final Map of Urban Extent for Kumasi, Ghana

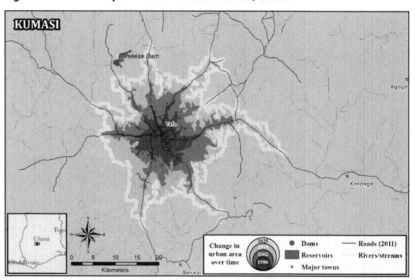

Table A4.1 Imagery Used to Classify Urban Extent for Each City and Each Time Period

Country	City	Target period	Path	Row	Date	Platform	Quality	UTM projection
Angola	Luanda	1990	182	66	6/30/91	Landsat 4-5 TM	Good	33N
Angola	Luanda	2000	182	66	6/14/00	Landsat 7	Good	33N
Angola	Luanda	2010	182	66	7/14/08	Landsat 5 TM	Good	33N
Benin	Cotonou	1990	191	56	12/27/90	n.a.	Poor - clouds	31N
Benin	Cotonou	1990	192	55	06/04/91	n.a.	Good	31N
Benin	Cotonou	1990	192	56	06/04/91	n.a.	Good	31N
Benin	Cotonou	2000	192	55	12/13/00	n.a.	Good	31N
Benin	Cotonou	2000	192	56	12/13/00	n.a.	Poor - opaque	31N
Benin	Cotonou	2000	191	56	12/09/01	n.a.	Good	31N
Benin	Cotonou	2010	191	56	10/02/11	n.a.	Poor - clouds + striping	31N
Benin	Cotonou	2010	192	55	12/12/11	n.a.	Poor - opaque + striping	31N
Benin	Cotonou	2010	192	56	12/12/11	n.a.	Poor - opaque + striping	31N
Burkina Faso	Ouagadougou	1990	195	51	9/10/90	Landsat 4-5 TM	Good	30N
Burkina Faso	Ouagadougou	2000	195	51	2/14/01	Landsat 7	Good	30N
Burkina Faso	Ouagadougou	2010	195	51	1/20/10	Landsat 5 TM	Good	30N
Cameroon	Douala	1990	186	57	12/21/86	n.a.	Good	32N
Cameroon	Douala	2000	186	57	12/17/99	n.a.	Poor - clouds	32N
Cameroon	Douala	2010	n.a.	n.a.	01/01/12	Bing Imagery	Not rated	32N
Cameroon	Yaoundé	1990	185	57	03/30/87	n.a.	Good	33N
Cameroon	Yaoundé	2000	185	57	05/18/00	n.a.	Good	33N
Cameroon	Yaoundé	2010	185	57	12/11/11	n.a.	Good	33N

(continued on next page)

Table A4.1 (continued)

Country	City	Target period	Path	Row	Date	Platform	Quality	UTM projection
Côte d'Ivoire	Abidjan	1990	196	56	12/24/88	n.a.	Poor - clouds	30N
Côte d'Ivoire	Abidjan	1990	195	56	01/02/89	n.a.	Good	30N
Côte d'Ivoire	Abidjan	2000	196	56	12/31/02	n.a.	Good	30N
Côte d'Ivoire	Abidjan	2000	195	56	02/26/03	n.a.	Poor - clouds	30N
Côte d'Ivoire	Abidjan	2010	195	56	01/15/11	n.a.	Poor - opaque + striping	30N
Côte d'Ivoire	Abidjan	2010	196	56	02/10/12	n.a.	Poor - opaque + striping	30N
Democratic Republic of Congo	Kinshasa	1990	182	63	01/10/87	n.a.	Poor - clouds	33N
Democratic Republic of Congo	Kinshasa	1990	182	63	08/09/94	n.a.	Poor - opaque + clouds	33N
Democratic Republic of Congo	Kinshasa	2000	182	63	09/02/00	n.a.	Poor - opaque + clouds	33N
Democratic Republic of Congo	Kinshasa	2000	182	63	04/30/01	n.a.	Good	33N

(continued on next page)

Table A4.1 (continued)

Country	City	Target period	Path	Row	Date	Platform	Quality	UTM projection
Democratic Republic of Congo	Kinshasa	2010	182	63	08/16/11	n.a.	Poor - clouds + striping	33N
Democratic Republic of Congo	Lubumbashi	1990	173	68	6/15/91	Landsat 4-5 TM	Good	35N
Democratic Republic of Congo	Lubumbashi	2000	173	68	5/1/01	Landsat 7	Good	35N
Democratic Republic of Congo	Lubumbashi	2010	173	68	7/2/09	Landsat 5 TM	Good	35N
Democratic Republic of Congo	Mbuji-Mayi	1990	176	64	9/8/91	Landsat 4-5 TM	Good	34N
Democratic Republic of Congo	Mbuji-Mayi	2000	176	64	6/7/01	Landsat 7	Good	34N
Democratic Republic of Congo	Mbuji-Mayi	2010	176	64	7/7/09	Landsat 5 TM	Good	34N

(continued on next page)

Table A4.1 (continued)

Country	City	Target period	Path	Row	Date	Platform	Quality	UTM projection
Ethiopia	Addis Ababa	1990	168	54	11/21/89	Landsat 4-5 TM	Good	37N
Ethiopia	Addis Ababa	2000	168	54	12/5/00	Landsat 7	Good	37N
Ethiopia	Addis Ababa	2010	168	54	1/10/11	Landsat 5 TM	Good	37N
Ghana	Accra	1990	193	56	01/10/91	n.a.	Poor - opaque	30N
Ghana	Accra	2000	193	56	12/26/02	n.a.	Good	30N
Ghana	Accra	2010	193	56	01/17/11	n.a.	Good	30N
Ghana	Kumasi	1990	194	55	01/11/86	n.a.	Good	30N
Ghana	Kumasi	2000	194	55	05/07/02	n.a.	Good	30N
Ghana	Kumasi	2010	194	55	02/06/10	n.a.	Good	30N
Guinea	Conakry	1990	202	53	12/24/90	Landsat 4-5 TM	Good	28N
Guinea	Conakry	2000	202	53	12/19/00	Landsat 7	Good	28N
Guinea	Conakry	2010	202	53	2/22/10	Landsat 5 TM	Good	28N
Kenya	Nairobi	1990	168	61	10/17/88	Landsat 4-5 TM	Good	37N
Kenya	Nairobi	2000	168	61	2/5/00	Landsat 7	Good	37N
Kenya	Nairobi	2010	168	61	8/19/10	Landsat 5 TM	Good	37N
Malawi	Blantyre	1990	167	71	7/1/89	Landsat 4-5 TM	Good	36N
Malawi	Blantyre	2000	167	71	5/26/02	Landsat 7	Good	36N
Malawi	Blantyre	2010	167	71	6/6/09	Landsat 5 TM	Good	36N
Malawi	Lilongwe	1990	168	70	5/11/91	Landsat 4-5 TM	Good	36N

(continued on next page)

Table A4.1 (continued)

Country	City	Target period	Path	Row	Date	Platform	Quality	UTM projection
Malawi	Lilongwe	2000	168	70	7/17/01	Landsat 7	Good	36N
Malawi	Lilongwe	2010	168	70	8/22/11	Landsat 5 TM	Good	36N
Mozambique	Maputo	1990	167	78	6/5/91	Landsat 4-5 TM	Good	36N
Mozambique	Maputo	2000	167	78	5/7/01	Landsat 7	Good	36N
Mozambique	Maputo	2010	167	78	9/7/08	Landsat 5 TM	Good	36N
Nigeria	Abuja	1990	189	54	12/21/87	n.a.	Good	32N
Nigeria	Abuja	2000	189	54	01/09/01	n.a.	Good	32N
Nigeria	Abuja	2010	189	54	01/18/10	n.a.	Good	32N
Nigeria	Ibadan	1990	191	55	04/12/86	n.a.	Good	30N
Nigeria	Ibadan	2000	191	55	02/06/00	n.a.	Poor - opaque	30N
Nigeria	Ibadan	2010	191	55	01/03/11	n.a.	Good	30N
Nigeria	Kano	1990	188	52	2/16/88	Landsat 4-5 TM	Good	32N
Nigeria	Kano	2000	188	52	10/28/99	Landsat 8	Good	32N
Nigeria	Kano	2010	NA	NA	1/1/12	Bing Imagery	Good	32N
Nigeria	Lagos	1990	191	55	12/18/84	n.a.	Good	31N
Nigeria	Lagos	1990	191	56	12/27/90	n.a.	Poor - clouds	31N
Nigeria	Lagos	1990	191	55	12/27/90	n.a.	Poor - clouds	31N
Nigeria	Lagos	2000	191	56	12/09/01	n.a.	Good	31N
Nigeria	Lagos	2000	191	55	12/09/01	n.a.	Good	31N
Nigeria	Lagos	2010	191	56	10/02/11	n.a.	Poor - clouds + striping	31N

(continued on next page)

181

Table A4.1 *(continued)*

Country	City	Target period	Path	Row	Date	Platform	Quality	UTM projection
Nigeria	Lagos	2010	191	55	01/06/12	n.a.	Poor - opaque + striping	31N
Republic of Congo	Brazzaville	1990	182	63	01/10/87	n.a.	Poor - clouds	33N
Republic of Congo	Brazzaville	2000	182	63	09/02/00	n.a.	Poor - opaque + clouds	33N
Republic of Congo	Brazzaville	2000	182	63	04/30/01	n.a.	Good	33N
Republic of Congo	Brazzaville	2010	182	63	08/16/11	n.a.	Poor - clouds + striping	33N
Senegal	Dakar	1990	205	50	10/15/89	Landsat 4-5 TM	Good	28N
Senegal	Dakar	2000	205	50	11/4/99	Landsat 7	Good	28N
Senegal	Dakar	2010	205	50	10/12/11	Landsat 5 TM	Good	28N
South Africa	Cape Town	1990	175	84	6/29/91	Landsat 4-5 TM	Good	34N
South Africa	Cape Town	2000	175	84	6/13/00	Landsat 7	Good	34N
South Africa	Cape Town	2010	175	84	4/17/11	Landsat 5 TM	Good	34N
South Africa	Durban	1990	168	81	4/9/91	Landsat 4-5 TM	Good	36N
South Africa	Durban	2000	168	81	6/28/00	Landsat 7	Good	36N
South Africa	Durban	2010	168	81	5/12/09	Landsat 5 TM	Good	36N
South Africa	Johannesburg	1990	170	78	5/6/90	Landsat 4-5 TM	Good	35N

(continued on next page)

Table A4.1 *(continued)*

Country	City	Target period	Path	Row	Date	Platform	Quality	UTM projection
South Africa	Johannesburg	2000	170	78	1/7/02	Landsat 7	Good	35N
South Africa	Johannesburg	2010	170	78	5/26/09	Landsat 5 TM	Good	35N
Sudan	Khartoum	1990	173	49	12/10/89	Landsat 4-5 TM	Good	36N
Sudan	Khartoum	2000	173	49	12/24/00	Landsat 7	Good	36N
Sudan	Khartoum	2010	173	49	1/26/10	Landsat 5 TM	Good	36N
Tanzania	Dar es Salaam	1990	166	65	12/09/89	n.a.	Poor - clouds	37N
Tanzania	Dar es Salaam	2000	166	65	02/09/01	n.a.	Poor - clouds	37N
Tanzania	Dar es Salaam	2010	166	65	07/01/09	n.a.	Good	37N
Uganda	Kampala	1990	171	60	2/27/89	Landsat 4-5 TM	Good	36N
Uganda	Kampala	2000	171	60	11/27/01	Landsat 7	Good	36N
Uganda	Kampala	2010	171	60	1/28/10	Landsat 5 TM	Good	36N
Zambia	Lusaka	1990	172	71	3/1/90	Landsat 4-5 TM	Good	35N
Zambia	Lusaka	2000	172	71	2/22/02	Landsat 7	Good	35N
Zambia	Lusaka	2010	172	71	5/30/11	Landsat 5 TM	Good	35N
Zimbabwe	Harare	1990	170	72	6/23/90	Landsat 4-5 TM	Good	36N
Zimbabwe	Harare	2000	170	72	9/30/00	Landsat 7	Good	36N
Zimbabwe	Harare	2010	170	72	5/26/09	Landsat 5 TM	Good	36N

Source: World Bank.

Note: In some cases, multiple images from slightly different dates were used to classify a single urban extent for a target period. n.a. = not available.

References

2030 Water Resources Group. 2009. *Charting Our Water Future; Economic Frameworks to Inform Decision-Making.* The 2030 Water Resources Group. http://www.2030waterresourcesgroup.com/water_full/Charting_Our_Water_Future_Final.pdf.

Africa Infrastructure Country Diagnostic (AICD). 2011. *Africa's Infrastructure: A Time for Transformation.* Accessed May 2012. African Development Bank Group, World Bank. Available at: http://www.infrastructureafrica.org/aicd/library/doc/552/africa's-infrastructure-time-transformation.

———. N.D. Datasets compiled by the World Bank and African Development Bank. Accessed May 2012. African Development Bank Group, World Bank. http://www.infrastructureafrica.org/.

African Development Bank (AfDB). 2004. *Nigeria Project Completion Report.* Ibadan Water Supply II Project. January.

———. 2005. *Yaoundé Sanitation Project (PADY).* Appraisal Report. Republic of Cameroon.

———. 2006. *Implementation of an Integrated Project of Water Supply and Sanitation Services for the Urban Poor in Kagugube Parish.* Appraisal Report. Central Division, Kampala, Uganda.

———. 2009. *Project Appraisal Report: Urban Water Supply and Sanitation for Oyo and Taraba States.* Nigeria.

————. 2010. *Urgent Water Supply and Sanitation Rehabilitation Project, Country: Zimbabwe.* Project Appraisal Report. Zimbabwe.

African Development Fund. 2007. *Appraisal Report—Angola.* Sumbe Water Supply, Sanitation, and Institutional Support Project, August 2007. Angola.

Alcamo, J. M., C. J. Vörösmarty, R. J. Naiman, D. P. Lettenmaier, and C. Pahl-Wostl. 2008. "A Grand Challenge for Freshwater Research: Understanding the Global Water System." *Environmental Research Letters* 3(1): 010202.

Allen, L., J. Christian-Schmith, and M. Palaniappan. 2010. "Overview of Greywater Reuse: The Potential of Greywater Systems to Aid Sustainable Water Management." Pacific Institute. Accessed May 2012. http://www.pacinst.org/reports/greywater_overview/greywater_overview.pdf.

Allen, R. G., L. S. Pereira, D. Raes, and M. Smith. 1998. "Crop Evapotranspiration—Guidelines for Computing Crop Water Requirements." *FAO Irrigation and Drainage,* Paper 56. Food and Agriculture Organization of the United Nations, Rome.

Anderson, J., and R. Iyaduri. 2003. "Integrated Urban Water Planning: Big Picture Planning Is Good for Wallet and the Environment." *Water Science and Technology* 47(7-8): 19–23.

Angel, S., J. Parent, D. L. Civco, and A. M. Blei. 2010. *Atlas of Urban Expansion.* Cambridge, MA: Lincoln Institute of Land Policy. Accessed May 2012. http://www.lincolninst.edu/subcenters/atlas-urban-expansion/.

Ashley, R., J. Blanksby, A. Cashman, L. Jack, G. Wright, J. Packman, L. Fewtrell, T. Poole, and C. Maksimovic. 2007. "Adaptable Urban Drainage: Addressing Change in Intensity, Occurrence and Uncertainty of Stormwater (AUDACIOUS)." *Built Environment* 33: 70–84.

Asian Development Bank (ADB). 2007. *Data Book of South East Asian Water Utilities 2005.* Manila: ADB. Accessed May 2012. http://www.adb.org/sites/default/files/pub/2007/SEAWUN-Data-Book.pdf.

————. 2007a. *2007 Benchmarking and Data Book of Water Utilities in India.* Manila: ADB. Accessed May 2012. http://www.scribd.com/drprasadbm/d/28792396-2007-Indian-Water-Utilities-Data-Book-1.

Athi Water Services Board (AWSB). 2012. *Feasibility Study and Master Plan for Developing New Water Sources for Nairobi and Satellite Towns.*

Awiti, A. 2012. "Kenya: Tackling Nairobi's Water Shortages." Op-ed. Nairobi, Kenya: *The Star,* April 30. Accessed May 2012. http://allafrica.com/stories/201205020066.html.

Bandura, R. 2008. "A Survey of Composite Indices Measuring Country Performances." UNDP/ODS Working Paper. Office of Development Studies, United Nations Development Programme, New York. http://web.undp.org/developmentstudies/docs/indices_2008_bandura.pdf.

Banerjee, S., and E. Morella. 2011. *Africa's Water and Sanitation Infrastructure: Access, Affordability and Alternatives.* Directions in Development, Infrastructure Series. Washington, DC: World Bank.

Banerjee, S., H. Skilling, V. Foster, C. Briceño-Garmendia, E. Morella, and T. Chfadi. 2008. "Ebbing Water, Surging Deficits: Urban Water Supply in Sub-Saharan Africa." Cross Country Annex. Africa Infrastructure Country Diagnostic (AICD), Phase 1. Background Paper 12. World Bank, Washington, DC.

Barrantes, G., and L. Gamez. 2007. "Programa de Pago de por Servicio Ambiental Hidrico de la Empresa de Servicios Publicos de Heredia." In *Ecomarkets: Costa Rica's Experience with Payments for Environmental Services,* eds. G. Platais and S. Pagiola. Washington, DC: World Bank.

Batchelor, C., C. Foneseca, and S. Smits. 2011. "Life-Cycle Costs of Rainwater Harvesting Systems." Occasional Paper 46. The Hague, Netherlands: IRC. Accessed May 2012. http://www.washdoc.info/docsearch/title/176546.

Biedler, M. 2012. "Integrated Urban Water Management for Douala, Cameroon." Background report. World Bank, Washington, DC.

Bieker, S., P. Cornel, and M. Wagner. 2010. "Semicentralised Supply and Treatment Systems: Integrated Infrastructure Solutions for Fast Growing Urban Areas." *Water Science and Technology: A Journal of the International Association on Water Pollution Research* 61(11): 2905–13.

Binney, P., A. Donald, V. Elmer, J. Ewert, O. Phillis, R. Skinner, and R. Young. 2010 "IWA Cities of the Future Program—Spatial Planning and Institutional Reform." Discussion Paper for the World Water Congress, September 2010. Accessed May 2012. http://www.iwahq.org/contentsuite/upload/iwa/document/updated%20iwa%20spatial%20planning%20and%20institutional%20reform%20group%20montreal%20discussion%20paper.pdf.

Bloch, R. 2012. *Integrating Urban Planning and Water Management in Sub-Saharan Africa.* Report No. J40252692. Birmingham: GHK Consultants. Paper produced for the World Bank, Washington, DC (available upon request from the authors).

Booysen, F. 2002. "An Overview and Evaluation of Composite Indices of Development." *Social Indicators Research* 59: 115–51.

Bremen Overseas Research and Development Association (BORDA). 2012. *Decentralized Wastewater Treatment Systems (DEWATS) and Sanitation in Developing Countries—A Practical Guide.* BORDA Publication.

Brown, R., N. Keath, and T. Wong. 2008. "Transitioning to Water Sensitive Cities: Historical, Current and Future Transition States." Proceedings of the 11th International Conference on Urban Drainage. Edinburgh, Scotland, UK.

Butterworth, J., P. McIntyre, and C. da Silva Wells. 2011. *SWITCH in the City: Putting Urban Water Management to the Test.* The Hague, Netherlands: SWITCH. Accessed May 2012. http://www.irc.nl/page/66812.

Carter, N., R. Kreutzwiser, and R. de Loe. 2005. "Closing the Circle: Linking Land Use Planning and Water Management at the Local Level." *Land Use Policy* 22: 115–17.

Chowdhury, S., and L. Squire. 2006. "Setting Weights for Aggregate Indices: An Application to the Commitment to Development Index and Human Development Index." *Journal of Development Studies* 42(5): 761–71.

Cities Alliance. 2008. "Stratégie de Développement Urbain de l'Agglomération de Cotonou." *Demographia 2011.* Demographia World Urban Areas. Accessed April 2011. http://www.citiesalliance.org/sites/citiesalliance.org/files/CAFiles/Projects/ACS_22.pdf.

Clarke, K. C., S. Hoppen, and L. Gaydos. 1997. "A Self-Modifying Cellular Automaton Model of Historical Urbanization in the San Francisco Bay Area." *Environment and Planning B: Planning and Design* 24: 247–61.

Closas, A., D. Shemie, and M. Jacobsen. Forthcoming. "Knowledge, Attitudes, and Practices Survey of Urban Water Management in Africa." World Bank, Washington, DC. Available at: http://water.worldbank.org/AfricaIUWM.

Cornell, P., A. Meda, and S. Bieker. 2011. "Wastewater as a Source of Energy, Nutrients, and Service Water." In *Treatise on Water Science, Volume 4,* ed. Peter Wilderer, 337–75. New York: Oxford Academic Press.

Cowater International. 2005. *District Town Sewerage /Sanitation Feasibility Study: Arua Master Plan.* Uganda: National Water and Sewerage Corporation.

Dasgupta, S., B. Laplante, S. Murray, and D. Wheeler. 2009. "Sea-Level Rise and Storm Surges: a Comparative Analysis of Impacts in Developing Countries." Policy Research Working Paper 4901. World Bank, Washington, DC.

Demographia. 2011. *Demographia World Urban Areas (World Agglomerations).* 7th ed. http://www.demographia.com/db-worldua.pdf.

Diacon, D. 1997. *Slum Networking: An Innovative Approach to Urban Development.* Coalville, Leicestershire, UK: Building and Social Housing Foundation.

Dillon, P., P. Pavelic, D. Page, H. Beringen, and J. Ward. 2009. *Managed Aquifer Recharge: An Introduction.* Waterlines Report Series: 13 (February). National Water Commission, Australian Government. Accessed May 2012. http://www.nwc.gov.au/__data/assets/pdf_file/0011/10442/Waterlines_MAR_completeREPLACE.pdf.

Dominguez-Torres, C. 2011. "Urban Access to Water Supply and Sanitation in Sub-Saharan Africa. Africa's Urban Transition: Implications for Water Management." Background paper. World Bank, Washington, DC.

Dominguez-Torres, C., and V. Foster. 2011. "The Central African Republic's Infrastructure: A Continental Perspective." Africa Infrastructure Country Diagnostic (AICD) Country Report. World Bank, Washington, DC. Accessed May 2012. https://openknowledge.worldbank.org/handle/10986/3461.

Donkor, S. M. K., and Y. E. Wolde. 2011. "Integrated Water Resources Management in Africa: Issues and Options." United Nations Economic Commission for Africa. Accessed May 2012. http://www.gdrc.org/uem/water/iwrm/iwrm-africa.pdf.

Droogers, P., and R. Allen. 2002. "Estimating Reference Evapotranspiration Under Inaccurate Data Conditions." *Irrigation and Drainage Systems* 16(1): 33–45.

Duncan, B., B. Blankespoor, and R. Engstrom. Forthcoming. "Urban Extent Map for 31 cities in Africa". World Bank, Washington, DC. Available at http://water.worldbank.org/AfricaIUWM.

Eckart, J., K. Ghebremichael, K. Khatri, H. Mutikanga, J. Sempewo, S. Tsegaye, and K. Vairavamoorthy. 2011. "Integrated Urban Water Management in Africa." Patel School of Global Sustainability, University of South Florida, Tampa. (Available upon request from the authors, World Bank.)

Eckart, J., K. Ghebremichael, K. Khatri, S. Tsegaye, and K. Vairavamoorthy. 2012. "Integrated Urban Water Management for Nairobi." Report prepared for the World Bank by Patel School of Global Sustainability, University of South Florida, Tampa. (Available upon request from the authors, World Bank.)

———. 2012a. "Integrated Urban Water Management for Mbale." Report prepared for the World Bank by Patel School of Global Sustainability, University of South Florida, Tampa. (Available upon request from the authors, World Bank.)

———. 2012b. "Integrated Urban Water Management for Arua." Report prepared for the World Bank by Patel School of Global Sustainability, University of South Florida, Tampa. (Available upon request from the authors, World Bank.)

Eckart, J., H. Sieker, and K. Vairavamoorthy. 2010. "Flexible Urban Drainage Systems." *Water Practice & Technology* 5(4). DOI:10.2166/wpt.2010.072.

The Economist Intelligence Unit and Siemens. 2011. *African Green City Index: Assessing the Environmental Performance of Africa's Major Cities.* http://www.siemens.com/entry/cc/en/greencityindex.htm.

Environmental Systems Research Institute (Esri). 2011. ArcGIS Desktop: Release 10. Redlands, CA: Esri.

Essandoh, H. M. K., C. Tizaoui, M. H. Mohamed, G. Amy, and D. Brdjanovic. 2009. "Soil Aquifer Treatment of Artificial Wastewater Under Saturated Conditions." *Water Research* 45(14): 4211–26.

European Commission (EC). 2002. *Common Implementation Strategy for the Water Framework Directive (2000/60/EC).* Guidance Document: 8. Public Participation in Relation to the Water Framework Directive. Accessed May

2012. http://ec.europa.eu/environment/water/water-framework/objectives/pdf/strategy2.pdf.

Foo, D. C. Y. 2007. "Water Cascade Analysis for Single and Multiple Impure Fresh Water Feed." *Chemical Engineering Research and Design* 85(8): 1169–77.

Foster, S., R. Hirata, S. Misra, and H. Garduno, H. 2010b. "Urban Groundwater Use Policy: Balancing the Benefits and Risks in Developing Nations." Strategic Overview Series No. 3. GW-MATE. World Bank, Washington, DC.

Foster, S., and A. Tuinhof. 2005. "The Role of Groundwater in the Water Supply of Greater Nairobi, Kenya." Case Profile Collection No. 13, GW-MATE. World Bank, Washington, DC.

Foster, S., A. Tuinhoff, and H. Garduno. 2006. "Groundwater Development in Sub-Saharan Africa: A Strategic Overview of Key Issues and Major Needs." Case Profile Collection No. 15. GW-MATE. World Bank, Washington, DC.

Foster, S., F. van Steenbergen, J. Zuleta, and H. Garduno. 2010a. "Conjunctive Use of Groundwater and Surface Water: from Spontaneous Coping Strategy to Adaptive Resource Management." Strategic Overview Series No. 2. GW-MATE. World Bank, Washington, DC.

Fred, N. 2011. Personal communication with municipal planner, Arua (during the field visit in Arua).

Gauff. 2011. "Arua Emergency Water Supply Project: Inception Report." Gauff Consulting Engineers. http://www.gauff.com/.

Giannini, A., M. Biasutti, I. M. Held, and A. H. Sobel. 2008. "A Global Perspective on African Climate." *Climatic Change* 90: 359–83.

Gleick, P. H. 2009. "Doing More with Less: Improving Water Use Efficiency Nationwide." *Southwest Hydrology* 8(1): 20–21.

Gleick, P. H., J. Christian-Smith, and H. Cooley. 2011. "Water-Use Efficiency and Productivity: Rethinking the Basin Approach." *Water International* 36(7): 784–98.

Global Water Intelligence (GWI). 2005. *Water Tariff Survey.* http://www.global-waterintel.com/.

———. 2009. "Bluewater Bio's South African Safari." 10(11) (November). http://www.globalwaterintel.com/archive/10/11/general/bluewater-bios-south-african-safari.html.

Global Water Partnership (GWP). 2010. "Towards a Water Secure World: What Is Integrated Water Resource Management." Accessed May 2012. http://www.gwp.org/The-Challenge/What-is-IWRM/.

Harrison, P. 2006. "On the Edge of Reason: Planning and Urban Futures in Africa." *Urban Studies* 43(2): 319–35.

Hijmans, R. J., S. E. Cameron, J. L. Parra, P. G. Jones, and A. Jarvis. 2005. "Very High Resolution Interpolated Climate Surfaces for Global Land Areas." *International Journal of Climatology* 25: 1965–78.

Hirji, R. 2012. Personal communication with Rafik Hirji, World Bank Senior Water Resources Specialist (who has worked on Nairobi water for more than a decade), Nairobi, Kenya.

Hove, M., and A. Tirimboi. 2011. "Assessment of Harare Water Service Delivery." *Journal of Sustainable Development in Africa* 13(4): 61–84.

Howe, C. A., J. Butterworth, I. K. Smout, A. M. Duffy, and K. Vairavamoorthy. 2011. *Sustainable Water Management in the City of the Future: Findings from the SWITCH Project 2006–2011.* SWITCH. http://www.switchurbanwater. eu/outputs/pdfs/SWITCH_-_Final_Report.pdf.

ICLEI—Local Governments for Sustainability. 2012. ICLEI Water. Accessed May 2012. http://www.iclei.org/.

————. 2012a. *Workshop Report: Options for IUWM in Nairobi, March 2012.* Report prepared for World Bank Africa IUWM project. Freiburg, Germany: ICLEI European Secretariat.

The International Benchmarking Network for Water and Sanitation Utilities (IBNET). 2012. Database. Accessed May 2012. http://www.ib-net.org/.

International Union for Conservation of Nature (IUCN) and United Nations Environment Programme (UNEP). 2010. The World Database on Protected Areas (WDPA). With World Conservation Monitoring Centre (WCMC). Cambridge, UK: UNEP-WCMC. Accessed May 2012. http://www. protectedplanet.net.

International Water Association (IWA). 2010. Cities of the Future Initiative. http://www.iwahq.org/66/events/iwa-events/2010/cities-of-the-future.html.

————. 2012. "Towards a Learning Alliance for Integrated Urban Water Management in Africa" (available upon request from the authors, World Bank).

IWA Water Wiki. 2011. *Durban eThekwini: Sanitation Status.* Accessed May 2012. http://www.iwawaterwiki.com/xwiki/bin/view/Articles/14%29+DURBAN+ THEKWINI+%28South+Africa%29+3.

————. 2012. *Decentralized Wastewater Treatment Systems for a Commune and Primary School: BORDA-Cambodia DEWATS Projects in Cambodia.* Accessed May 2012. http://www.iwawaterwiki.org/xwiki/bin/view/Articles/5Decentra lizedWastewaterTreatmentSystemsforaCommuneandPrimarySchool- BORDA-CambodiaDEWATSProjectsinCambodia.

Japan International Cooperation Agency (JICA). 2012. *Development Study for Urban Rehabilitation Plan in Kinshasa.* Accessed May 2012. http://gwweb. jica.go.jp/km/ProjectView.nsf/VWAEPrint/E7503F0C85FE3CE2492575 D100360177.

Jarvis, A., H. I. Reuter, A. Nelson, and E. Guevara. 2008. *Hole-Filled SRTM for the Globe Version 4.* (Available from the CGIAR-CSI SRTM 90m database.) Accessed May 2012. http://srtm.csi.cgiar.org.

Kessides, C. 2006. "The Urban Transition in Sub-Saharan Africa: Implications for Economic Growth and Poverty Reduction." Africa Region Working Paper Series 97. Washington, DC: Cities Alliance.

Khatri, K., and K. Vairavamoorthy. 2007. "Challenges for Urban Water Supply and Sanitation in the Developing Countries." Paper prepared for the Symposium on Water for Changing World-Enhancing Local Knowledge and Capacity, June 13–15. Delft: UNESCO-IHE Institute for Water Education.

Kraay, A., and N. Tawara. 2010 "Can Disaggregated Indicators Identify Governance Reform Priorities?" World Bank, Washington, DC. Accessed May 2012. https://openknowledge.worldbank.org/handle/10986/3746.

Lahnsteiner, J., G. Lempert, I. S. Kim, J. Cho, and S. Kim, S. 2007. "Water Management in Windhoek, Namibia." *Water Science & Technology* 55(1-2): 441–48.

Landis, J. 2001. "CUF, CUFII, and CURBA: A Family of Spatially Explicit Urban Growth and Land-Use Policy Simulation Models." In *Planning Support Systems, Integrating Geographic Information Systems, Models and Visualization Tools,* ed. R. Brail and R. Klosterman, 157–200. Redlands, CA: EsRI Press.

Lee, E., and K. Schwab. 2005. "Deficiencies in Drinking Water Distribution Systems in Developing Countries." *Journal of Water and Health* 3(2): 109–127.

Lehner, B., C. R. Liermann, C. Revenga, C. Vörösmarty, B. Fekete, P. Crouzet P. Döll, M. Endejan, K. Frenken, J. Magome, C. Nilsson, J. Robertson, R. Rödel, N. Sindorf, and D. Wisser. 2011. "High Resolution Mapping of the World's Reservoirs and Dams for Sustainable River Flow Management." *Frontiers in Ecology and the Environment* 9(9): 494–502.

Lehner, B., K. Verdin, and A. Jarvis. 2008. "New Global Hydrography Derived from Spaceborne Elevation Data." *Eos, Transactions, AGU* 89(10): 93–94.

Lusaka City Council. 2003. Strategic Municipal Solid Waste Management Plan for Lusaka City.

MacDonald, A.M., H.C. Bonsor, R.C. Calow, R.G. Taylor, D.J. Lapworth, L. Maurice, J. Tucker, and B.É. ÓDochartaigh. 2011. *Groundwater Resilience to Climate Change in Africa.* British Geological Survey Open Report, OR/11/031: 25.

Maheepala, S., J. Blackmore, C. Diaper, M. Moglia, A. Sharma, and S. Kenway. 2010. *Manual for Adopting Integrated Urban Water Management for Planning.* Denver, CO: Water Research Foundation. Accessed May 2012. http://espace.uq.edu.au/view/UQ:215523.

Maoulidi, M. 2010. *A Water and Sanitation Needs Assessment for Kumasi, Ghana.* MCI Social Sector Working Paper Series: 16.

Marchal, V., R. Dellink, D. van Vuuren, C. Clapp, J. Château, B. Magné, and J. van Vliet. 2011. *OECD Environmental Outlook to 2050.* Accessed May 2012. http://www.oecd.org/dataoecd/32/53/49082173.pdf.

Marsden, J., and P. Pickering. 2006. "Securing Australia's Urban Water Supplies: Opportunities and Impediments." Marsden-Jacob Associates. Accessed May 2012. http://www.watercentre.org/resources/search-resources/Securing_Australia_Urban_Wate_SuppliesMarsdenJacob.pdf.

Martin, S., and R. Puddy. 2012. "Go With the Flow: States Unite to Sink Murray-Darling Plan." *The Australian*, April 17. Accessed May 2012. http://www.theaustralian.com.au/in-depth/murray-darling-crisis/go-with-the-flow-states-unite-to-sink-murray-darling-plan/story-e6frg6px-1226328230840.

McCluskey, D., J. Duncan, B. Blankespoor, and M. Naughton. Forthcoming. "Maps and Box Plots of Future Climate and Hydrologic Indicators for 31 Cities in Africa." World Bank, Washington, DC. Available at: http://water.worldbank.org/AfricaIUWM.

McGrath, M. 2012. "Huge Water Resource Exists Under Africa." *BBC World Service*, April 20. Accessed May 2012. http://www.bbc.co.uk/news/science-environment-17775211.

McKinsey. 2011. *Urban World: Mapping the Economic Power of Cities.* Accessed May 2012. http://www.mckinsey.com/insights/mgi/research/urbanization/urban_world.

Milly, P. C. D., J. Betancourt, M. Falkenmark, R. Hirsch, Z. Kundzewicz, D. Lettenmaier, and R. Stouffer. 2008. "Stationarity Is Dead—Whither Water Management?" *Science* 1(319): 573–74.

Mitchell, T. D., T. D. Carter, P. D. Jones, M. Hulme, and M. New. 2003. "A Comprehensive Set of High-Resolution Grids of Monthly Climate for Europe and the Globe: The Observed Record (1901–2000) and 16 Scenarios (2001–2100)." *Journal of Climate* (submitted).

Mitchell, V. G. 2004. "Integrated Urban Water Management: A Review of Current Australian Practice. *CSIRO & AWA Report*: CMIT-2004-075.

Moffitt, L. J., N. Zirogiannis, and A. Danilenko. 2012. "Developing a Robust Water Utility Vulnerability Index." *Water Asset Management International* 8(1): 6–11.

Morel, A., and S. Diener. 2006. *Greywater Management in Low and Middle-Income Countries, Review of Different Treatment Systems for Households or Neighbourhoods.* Dubendorf, Switzerland: Swiss Federal Institute of Aquatic Science and Technology (Eawag). Accessed May 2012. http://www.eawag.ch/forschung/sandec/publikationen/ewm/dl/Morel_Diener_Greywater_2006_lowres.pdf.

Mtethiwa, A. H., A. Munyenyembe, W. Jere, and E. Nyali. 2008. "Efficiency of Oxidation Ponds in Wastewater Treatment." *International Journal of Environmental Research* 2(2): 149–52.

Mugabi, J., and V. Castro. 2009. *Water Operators Partnerships—Africa Utility Performance Assessment.* Water Operators Partnership. Accessed 2012. http://www.unhabitat.org/downloads/docs/WOP_Report.pdf.

Muller, M. 2010. "Fit for Purpose: Taking Integrated Water Resource Management Back to Basics." *Irrigation and Drainage Systems* 24(3-4): 161–75.

National Water and Sewerage Corporation (NWSC). 2012. Personal communication with staff and M. Christopher, Area Manager Arua Office, Uganda: NWSC.

Naughton, M., A. Closas, and M. Jacobsen. Forthcoming. "IUWM Challenges and Capacities Index." World Bank, Washington, DC. Available at: http://water.worldbank.org/AfricaIUWM.

Open Street Map. 2011. Packaged by CloudMade. Accessed May 2012. http://downloads.cloudmade.com/africa.

Organisation for Economic Co-operation and Development (OECD). 2007. *Côte d'Ivoire, Perspectives Economiques en Afrique.* Paris: OECD.

———. 2008. *Handbook on Constructing Composite Indicators.* Paris: OECD. Accessed 2012. http://www.oecd.org/dataoecd/37/42/42495745.pdf.

Otterpohl, R., U. Braun, and M. Oldenburg. 2003. "Innovative Technologies for Decentralised Water, Wastewater and Biowaste Management in Urban and Peri-Urban Areas." *Water Science and Technology* 48(11-12): 23–32.

Parrot, L. J. Sotamenou, and B. K. Dia. 2009. "Municipal Solid Waste Management in Africa: Strategies and Livelihoods in Yaoundé, Cameroon." *Waste Management* 29: 986–95.

Parry, M. L., O. F. Canziani, J. P. Palutikof, P. J. Van der Linden, and C. E. Hanson, eds. 2007. *Contribution of Working Group II to the Fourth Assessment Report of the 2007 Intergovernmental Panel on Climate Change.* Cambridge, UK and New York, NY: Cambridge University Press. Accessed May 2012. http://www.ipcc.ch/publications_and_data/ar4/wg2/en/contents.html.

Peter-Varbanets, M., C. Zurbrügg, C. Swartz, and W. Pronk. 2009. "Review: Decentralized Systems for Potable Water and the Potential of Membrane Technology." *Water Research* 43(2): 245–65.

Pinsent Masons. 2012. *Pinsent Masons Water Yearbook 2011–2012.* http://water-yearbook.pinsentmasons.com/.

Potts, D. 2012. "Whatever Happened to Africa's Urbanization?" African Research Institute. http://www.africaresearchinstitute.org/files/counterpoints/docs/Whatever-happened-to-Africas-rapid-urbanisation-6PZXYPRMW7.pdf.

Pravettoni, R., and UNEP/GRID-Arendal. 2011. *Slum Population in Africa.* Accessed May 2012. http://www.grida.no/graphicslib/detail/slum-population-in-urban-africa_d7d6.

Rees, J. 2006. "Urban Water and Sanitation Services: An IWRM Approach." TEC Background Papers, No. 11. Global Water Partnership, Stockholm, Sweden.

Rekacewicz, P. 2006. "Global Water Stress and Scarcity." *Vital Water Graphics 2.* UNEP/GRID-Arendal. http://www.grida.no/graphicslib/detail/global-water-stress-and-scarcity_14bc.

República de Mozambique, Ministerio de Obras Publicas, and FIPAG. 2011. *Maputo Water Supply Project, Master Plan Main Report.* Republica de Mozambique.

Repúblique du Congo. 2010. *Analyse de la Situation et Estimation des Besoins en Sante et Environnement dans le Cadre de la Mise en Oeuvre de la Declaration de Libreville, Rapport National.* Republique du Congo.

Reymond, P., O. Cofie, L. Raschid, and D. Kone. 2009. "Design Considerations and Constraints in Applying On-Farm Wastewater Treatment for Urban Agriculture." SWITCH. Accessed May 2012. http://www.switchurbanwater. eu/outputs/pdfs/w5-2_cacc_pap_design_considerations_and_constraints_ for_on-farm_wastewater_treatment.pdf.

Rieck, C., and P. Onyango. 2010. "Public Toilet with Biogas Plant and Water Kiosk, Naivasha, Kenya." Sustainable Sanitation Alliance (SuSanA), Eschborn. Accessed May 2012. http://www.sswm.info/library/1242.

Ruden, F. 2007. "The Discovery of a Regional Neogene Aquifer in Coastal Tanzania," *Coastal Aquifers: Challenges and Solutions* 1: 363–72.

Rural Focus Ltd. 2011. "Inventory of all Boreholes Drilled Within Nairobi Metropolitan, Kenya." http://www.wrma.or.ke/index.php?option=com_conte nt&task=view&id=192&Itemid=318.

Santé, I., A. M. Garcia, D. Miranda, and R. Crecente. 2010. "Cellular Automata Models for the Simulation of Real-World Urban Processes: A Review and Analysis." *Landscape and Urban Planning* 96(2): 108–22.

Schneider, A., M. A. Friedl, and D. Potere. 2009. "A New Map of Global Urban Extent from MODIS Data." *Environmental Research Letters* 4: Art. 044003.

Sen, S. 2012. *Waste Water, Drainage, and Solid Waste Management for Africa.* Background paper for IUWM study. World Bank, Washington, DC. (Available upon request from the authors, World Bank.)

Sharma, S. K., and K. Vairavamoorthy. 2009. "Urban Water Demand Management: Prospects and Challenges for the Developing Countries." *Water and Environment Journal* 23(3): 210–18.

Smith, M., and M. Cartin. 2011. *Water Vision to Action: Catalyzing Change through the IUCN Water and Nature Initiative: Results Report.* Gland, Switzerland: IUCN Water and Nature Initiative.

Standard Bank of South Africa. 2011. "Africa Macro: Insight and Strategy, The Five Trends Powering Africa's Ensuring Allure. Trend 2: Africa's Transformational Urban Swell." Accessed May 2012. https://m.research.standardbank. com/Research?view=1671-222B0798E5AA49A1B28E2629C756BCAA-1.

Strzepek, K., A. McCluskey, B. Boehlert, M. Jacobsen, and C. Fant. 2011. "Climate Variability and Change: A Basin Scale Indicator Approach to Understanding the Risks to Water Resources Management and Development." Water Paper. World Bank, Washington, DC. Accessed May 2012. http://water.worldbank. org/publications/climate-variability-and-change-basin-scale-indicator-approach-understanding-risk-water.

Strzepek, K. M., and C. W. Fant IV. 2010. *Water and Climate Change: Modeling the Impact of Climate Change on Hydrology and Water Availability.* University of Colorado and Massachusetts Institute of Technology.

Sustainable Water Management Improves Tomorrow's Cities Health (SWITCH). 2011. *SWITCH: Managing Water for the City of the Future.* Accessed May 2012. SWITCH. http://www.switchurbanwater.eu/.

———. 2011a. "Managing Water for the City of the Future. Learning Alliances: Introduction." SWITCH. Accessed May 2012. http://www.switchurbanwater. eu/la_intro.php.

Tan, P. L. 2006 "Legislating for Adequate Public Participation in Allocating Water in Australia." *Water International* 31(4): 455–71.

Tettey-Lowor, F. 2009. "Closing the Loop between Sanitation and Agriculture in Accra, Ghana: Improving Yields in Urban Agriculture by Using Urine as a Fertilizer and Drivers & Barriers for Scaling-up." MSc thesis. Wageningen University, the Netherlands.

Tucci, C., J. A. Goldenfum, and J. N. Parkinson. 2009. *Integrated Urban Water Management: Humid Tropics.* Urban Water Series. UNESCO-IHP, Tailor and Francis, CRC Press.

Tuinhof, A., and J. Heederik. 2003. "Management of Aquifer Recharge and Subsurface Storage." Netherlands National Committee—International Association of Hydrogeologists. http://siteresources.worldbank.org/INTWRD/ Resources/GWMATE_Final_booklet.pdf.

UNESCO-IHP. 2009. *Integrated Urban Water Management: Humid Tropics,* ed. J. Parkinson, J. Goldenfum, and C. Tucci. Paris: UNESCO.

UN-Habitat. 2006. *State of the World's Cities 2006/2007: The Millennium Development Goals and Urban Sustainability.* London: Earthscan.

———. 2007. *Profil Urbain de Ouagadougou.* Nairobi: UN-Habitat.

———. 2007a. *Zambia: Lusaka Urban Profile.* Nairobi: UN-Habitat.

———. 2008. *The State of African Cities: A Framework for Addressing Urban Challenges in Africa.* Nairobi: UN-Habitat.

————. 2010. *Solid Waste Management in the World's Cities: Water and Sanitation in the World's Cities 2010*. Nairobi: UN-Habitat.

————. 2011. *State of the World's Cities 2010/2011: Bridging the Urban Divide*. Nairobi: UN-Habitat..

————. 2011a. *Green Hills, Blue Cities: An Ecosystems Approach to Water Resources Management for African Cities*. Nairobi: UN-Habitat.

————. 2012. *Global Urban Observatory Statistics*. Nairobi: UN-Habitat. Accessed May 2012. http://ww2.unhabitat.org/programmes/guo/statistics.asp.

United Nations Department of Economic and Social Affairs (UNDESA). 2010. *World Urbanization Prospects: The 2009 Revision*. UNDESA, New York, NY. http://esa.un.org/unpd/wup/Documentation/highlights.htm.

————. 2011. *World Population Prospects: The 2010 Revision*. UNDESA, New York, NY. http://esa.un.org/unpd/wpp/index.htm.

————. 2012. *World Urbanization Prospects: The 2011 Revision*. UNDESA, New York, NY. Accessed May 2012. http://esa.un.org/unpd/wup/Documentation/highlights.htm.

United Nations Environment Programme (UNEP). 2008. *Atlas of Our Changing Environment (from Landsat Imagery)*. UNEP, Nairobi, Kenya. Accessed May 2012. http://www.unep.org/dewa/africa/africaAtlas/PDF/en/TOC.pdf.

————. 2010. *Africa Water Atlas*. UNEP, Nairobi, Kenya. Accessed May 2012. http://www.unep.org/publications/contents/pub_details_search.asp?ID=4165.

United Nations Statistics Division (UNSD). 2011. *UNSD Environmental Indicators*. UNSD, New York, NY. http://unstats.un.org/unsd/environment/qindicators.htm.

Universal Water Consultants Ltd. 2011. *Hydrological Survey Report: Seven Boreholes in Arua*. Prepared for the National Water and Sewerage Corporation, Arua Branch.

Vairavamoorthy, K., S. Gorantiwar, and A. Pathirana. 2008. "Managing Urban Water Supplies in Developing Countries—Climate Change and Water Scarcity Scenarios." *Physics and Chemistry of the Earth* 33(5): 330–39.

Vairavamoorthy, K., J. M. Yan, S. D. Gorantiwar, and H. Galgale. 2007. "Modelling the Risk of Contaminant Intrusion in Water Mains." *ICE Journal of Water Management* 160(2): 123–32.

Vairavamoorthy, K., Y. Zhou, and M. Mansoor. 2009. "Urban Water Systems and Their Interactions." *Desalination* 251: 402–09.

Van der Merwe, B. 2000. "Integrated Water Resource Management in Windhoek, Namibia." *Water Supply: The Review Journal of the International Water Supply Association* 18(1): 376–81.

van Ginneken, M., U. Netterstrom, and A. Bennett. 2012. *More, Better, or Different Spending? Trends in Public Expenditure on Water and Sanitation in Sub-Saharan Africa.* Washington, DC: World Bank.

Waddell, P. 2002. "UrbanSim: Modeling Urban Development for Land Use, Transportation and Environmental Planning." *Journal of the American Planning Association* 68(3): 297–314.

Wang X. C., R. Chen, Q. H. Zhang, and K. Li. 2008. "Optimized Plan of Centralized and Decentralized Wastewater Reuse Systems for Housing Development in the Urban Area of Xi'an, China." *Water Science & Technology* 58(5): 969–75.

Water and Sanitation Program. 2012. *Africa: Economics of Sanitation Initiative.* World Bank, Washington, DC. Accessed May 2012. http://www.wsp.org/wsp/content/africa-economic-impacts-sanitation.

Wegener, M. 1998. *The IRPUD Model: Overview.* Dortmund: Institute of Spatial Planning, University of Dortmund.

WHO/UNICEF. 2010. *Progress on Sanitation and Drinking Water.* World Health Organization and United Nations Children's Fund.

———. 2012. *Progress on Drinking Water and Sanitation, 2012 Update.* Joint Monitoring Programme, World Health Organization and United Nations Children's Fund. Accessed May 2012. http://www.unicef.org/media/files/JMPreport2012.pdf.

World Bank. 2005. "Climate Variability and Water Resources Degradation in Kenya." Working paper. World Bank, Washington, DC.

———. 2006. World Bank Open Data Catalog. http://data.worldbank.org/indicator/NY.GDP.PCAP.CD?page=1.

———. 2007. "Project Appraisal Document to the Federal Democratic Republic of Ethiopia for an Urban Water Supply and Sanitation Project." March 29. Report 39119-ET. World Bank, Washington, DC.

———. 2008. "Project Appraisal Document to the Republic of Congo for an Urban Water Supply Project." Report No. 46545. World Bank, Washington, DC.

———. 2009. *Urbanization and Growth, Commission on Growth and Development.* Washington, DC: World Bank.

———. 2009a. "Project Appraisal Document to Burkina Faso for an Urban Water Sector Project," April 30. Report 47392-BF. World Bank, Washington, DC.

———. 2009b. "Lagos Metropolitan Development and Governance Project (LMDGP) Solid Waste Management Component, Environmental & Social Impact Assessment ESIA, Final Report." World Bank, Washington, DC.

———. 2010. "Integrated Urban Water Management: An Operational Framework for Stronger World Bank Engagement in Latin America." Draft. December 8. World Bank, Washington, DC.

———. 2010a. *World Development Indicators 2010*. Washington, DC: World Bank.

———. 2010b. "République du Benin: Analyse Environnementale Pays." Rapport 58190-BJ. World Bank, Washington, DC.

———. 2010c. "Report on the Status of Disaster Risk Reduction in Africa." World Bank, Washington, DC. Accessed May 2012. http://www.gfdrr.org/gfdrr/sites/gfdrr.org/files/publication/AFR.pdf.

———. 2011. "Strategic Analysis of Water Resources Investments in Kenya. Water Resources Management (AFTWR), Africa Region." Water Partnership Program. World Bank, Washington, DC.

———. 2011a. "Water Resources Management in an Urban Context in Africa." Draft report. World Bank, Washington, DC. (Available upon request from the authors, World Bank.)

———. 2011b. "Water Management in Tegucigalpa." Unpublished draft. November 2011. World Bank, Washington, DC.

———. 2011c. "Implementation Completion and Results Report to the United Republic of Tanzania for a Dar Es Salaam Water Supply and Sanitation Project." Report ICR00001361. World Bank, Washington, DC.

———. 2011d. "Africa's Future and the World Bank's Role to Support It." World Bank, Washington, DC. Accessed May 2012. http://siteresources.worldbank.org/INTAFRICA/Resources/AFR_Regional_Strategy_3-2-11.pdf.

———. 2012. "Do Middle Classes Bring Institutional Reforms?" Policy Research Working Paper 6015. World Bank, Washington, DC. Accessed May 2012. http://ftp.iza.org/dp6430.pdf.

———. 2012a. *Planning, Connecting, and Financing Cities—Now. Urbanization Review Flagship Report*. (Forthcoming.) Washington, DC: World Bank.

———. 2012b. "Background Paper on Time to Act: Achieving Flood Resilience in African Cities." World Bank, Washington, DC. (Available upon request from the authors, World Bank.)

———. 2012c. "Water Management and Development Project P123204." Project Information Document, Report PIDC351. World Bank, Washington, DC.

World Health Organization (WHO). 2006. *Cholera Update Northern Sudan 8 October 2006*. Geneva: WHO.

———. 2008. *Advocacy, Communication and Social Mobilization for TB Control: A Guide to Developing Knowledge, Attitude and Practice Surveys*. Geneva: WHO.

———. 2008a. *The Global Burden of Disease: 2004 Update*. Geneva: WHO.

———. 2011. *Regional Humanitarian Health Update, Eastern and Southern Africa, May 2011*. Geneva: WHO.